HOMESCHOOLING

A Research-Based How-To Manual

Andrea D. Clements

ScarecrowEducation
Lanham, Maryland • Toronto • Oxford
2004

Published in the United States of America
by ScarecrowEducation
An imprint of The Rowman & Littlefield Publishing Group, Inc.
4501 Forbes Boulevard, Suite 200, Lanham, Maryland 20706
www.scaecroweducation.com

PO Box 317
Oxford
OX2 9RU, UK

British Library Cataloguing in Publication Information Available

Library of Congress Cataloging-in-Publication Data

Clements, Andrea D., 1961–
    Homeschooling : a research-based how-to manual / Andrea D. Clements.
        p. cm.
    Includes bibliographical references and index.
    ISBN 1-57886-128-4 (pbk. : alk. paper)
1. Home schooling—Handbooks, manuals, etc. I. Title: Home schooling.
II. Title.
LC40.C56 2004
370.04'2—dc22   2004003338

∞™ The paper used in this publication meets the minimum requirements of
American National Standard for Information Sciences—Permanence of
Paper for Printed Library Materials, ANSI/NISO Z39.48-1992.
Manufactured in the United States of America.

CONTENTS

PREFACE

Another "how to homeschool your children" book may seem unnecessary, but this one is different. After teaching at the college level for more than fifteen years, teaching a college-level course for homeschooling parents for the past five years, and having homeschooled children of my own for over five years, I have seen the need for a more research-based look at issues surrounding homeschooling. As a faculty member in the College of Education at a moderately sized public university, I am well acquainted with educational research. So much research has been done on learning, teaching, and classroom management that it seems a waste not to glean what we can from the results of all that work. I teach a college course particularly geared toward parents who are currently homeschooling their children, but it is often taken by parents who are considering homeschooling as well as other educators. As a part of the course, I have attempted to take material from learning theory, educational psychology, developmental psychology, and motivation theory and apply it to homeschooling. The course has been so popular, and the homeschooling parents I've come in contact with have been so eager for the information, that I decided to put it in book form. My aim is to make the information readable and useful, but also to base it on research findings rather than just use anecdotal examples.

When I teach research methods to my undergraduate and graduate students, I try to convince them to be skeptical of opinions and poorly done research. I have attempted to be the skeptic for the audience of this book and report the most trustworthy and effective findings.

My intent is not to convince anyone to homeschool. In fact, it is geared to those who have already decided to homeschool and are trying to decide how to go about it. The book will also be helpful for those who want a realistic look at the amount of work that goes into homeschooling and the types of decisions that must be made before deciding whether or not to homeschool. Rather than make the decisions for the reader, I have provided information and suggested applications, but will leave the final decisions up to each reader. Critiques of public or private schools and explanations of the benefits of homeschooling are beyond the scope of the book, as are the legal requirements of homeschooling.

ACKNOWLEDGMENTS

My most sincere thanks go to my husband, Dale, and my children, Tanner, Tori, Timothy, and Tucker, who have been very patient and helpful throughout the preparation of this book. Without children to home-school, I'd have no expertise in the area, and without a husband willing to stay home and oversee the schoolwork, we would not have been able to homeschool. This book is dedicated to them.

Jan Brownlee, an excellent proofreader, fine grammarian, and great friend who is willing to make suggestions and question me, has raised this book to a higher level of quality. There are no words that can express how thankful I am for her help or how perfectly her skills met my needs in the writing of this book.

INTRODUCTION

Topics covered within this book include learning, personality character-istics, choosing curriculum (or not), motivation, discipline, testing, learn-ing environments, and scheduling. While none is covered exhaustively, vast amounts of research and experience have been boiled down to a fairly simple summary of each topic and applications have been given. This information can be used to make informed decisions regarding homeschooling, private schooling, and public schooling, and it may even apply in other settings such as dealings with colleagues and social ac-quaintances. Information has been related to homeschooling through-out, but other applications have been inserted when appropriate.

What is known or thought about how people learn has been included early in this book. There are various views of how learning happens, and each parent's particular view will influence many decisions about home-schooling. For example, if someone believes that a topic has to be ex-plained by an adult before it can be learned, then he or she would most likely not choose a curriculum for his or her child that is primarily self-study. Several theories of how children learn are explained, and the strengths and weaknesses are highlighted so that parents can decide which elements of that theory would be useful as they set out to teach. Examples and applications are given throughout.

The subject of academic ability has also been covered. Academic ability in this context refers to intelligence and amount of prior learning. Both have an impact on what materials and teaching methods can be used and how rapidly material can be covered. Differing views of intelligence have been described, as have methods of intelligence testing. The intelligence of a child, and the intelligence of a homeschooling parent, can affect what types of curriculum materials and teaching methods can be used effectively, as well as what type of time commitment must be made for homeschooling. The impact of prior learning (including material learned in earlier school experiences, previous homeschooling, or learning acquired in nonschool settings) has been included as well. Differences in prior learning among students in a traditional class are quite difficult for a classroom teacher to accommodate, but they can be readily accommodated when homeschooling.

Personality characteristics of both the student(s) and the parent(s) who will teach have been addressed. These characteristics include temperament (e.g., typical mood, tendency to follow a schedule, tendency to take risks) and learning style (how one learns best or most naturally). It is important before homeschooling to "diagnose" everyone involved in terms of personality characteristics. While I don't believe there are particular personality types that cannot be homeschooling parents or cannot be homeschooled children, some combinations are more challenging than others. Accommodations can be made if these challenges are known ahead of time.

Issues such as ways to motivate and discipline children have been covered, as well as how to best set up the physical environment for homeschooling. As a self-acknowledged efficiency fanatic, streamlining the homeschooling process is a goal for me. If children do not have to search for their materials, they will get more work done and have less opportunity to get into trouble.

One of the most thoroughly covered topics within this book is how to choose curriculum materials, or what will be taught, or whether *materials* will be used at all. In fact, decisions that factor into the ultimate decision of what to teach have been discussed throughout the book because so many of the other topics relate to this decision. An example of a type of decision that must be made before committing to a particular type of instructional material would be how deeply or how rapidly topics will be covered. Other considerations include how much hands-on teaching time the parent will take with the child; whether and how testing will be done; and the results of the diagnoses of intelligence, prior learning, temperament, and learning styles discussed earlier.

As mentioned, this is a how-to book, but those "how-to's" have been drawn from a very extensive base of research findings in the fields of educational psychology, learning theory, developmental psychology, and motivation theory. The aim is to make the material easy to understand but convincing. On to the task at hand.

THEORIES OF LEARNING

One of the most compelling questions asked by educators is how learning occurs. Just as with anything we do not completely understand, there are a multitude of theories. As my students often hear, "If I knew which theory was correct, that would be the only one I would need to teach." The attempt in this chapter is to describe the most popular theories of learning in very simple terms and to informally critique them by highlighting research that either supports or refutes them.

PIAGET'S COGNITIVE DEVELOPMENTAL THEORY

In the 1920s, Jean Piaget (Piaget and Inhelder, 1969) theorized about how children learn as he studied his own children. Although that process may not be the most respected way to develop a theory, many of his ideas continue to some extent to explain children's learning. Although entire books have been written on Piaget's ideas, only the highlights are given in this chapter. Three main concepts in his learning theory are organization, equilibration, and progression through predictable stages of cognitive development. In other words, he thought that children's thinking changed in predictable ways as they grew. *Organization* and *progression through stages* have to do with how the actual learning takes place and is discussed in this chapter. *Equilibration* concerns the motivation for learning and is discussed in the chapter on motivation.

Organization

According to Piaget, children will basically seek what is good and automatically attempt to explore and to organize new information they encounter. This causes them to improve their amount of knowledge and their efficient use of that knowledge. There are some central terms related to this idea of organization.

Schemes. Schemes are mental *structures* people construct to organize their knowledge. For example, a child may have a scheme for doing long division, a scheme for how to ride a bicycle, a scheme for how to take notes in a class, a scheme for what a mammal is, and so forth. As a child gets older and is faced with more and more information, the number and complexity of schemes increases. This happens, according to Piaget, through *adaptation*, which can take the form of either *assimilation* or *accommodation*.

Adaptation. Adaptation is what takes place when someone is presented with some kind of new information. If the information is new, it has not yet been included in a scheme, and therefore adaptation of one kind or the other must occur. If there is a scheme that already fits the new information, the new information can be classified under that existing scheme. This is called *assimilation.* For example, a baby bangs anything it holds against the high-chair tray. The baby is given a new object that is immediately banged on the high chair tray. Assimilation has occurred. When completing schoolwork, assimilation could take the form of sounding out new words. Every time the student comes upon a new word, the letters are sounded out. This might be quite functional for reading. However, approaching every math problem the same way (division the same as addition) would not result in the same level of success.

If there is no existing scheme that fits the new information, *accommodation* must occur. This means that an existing scheme must be modified or a new scheme developed. For example, the baby in the previous example is handed a raw egg. The baby bangs the egg and it breaks.

Now the baby must accommodate his or her scheme by not banging white, oval objects.

Accommodation in a school setting could be in the form of modifying study habits when taking a new course that requires more memorization than previous courses. Piaget's idea of *organization* was that through the process of assimilation and accommodation, schemes are used, added, and modified in order to organize information.

Piaget's Cognitive Developmental Stages

Piaget theorized that all children pass through four stages, ending in adult-like thinking by the teen years. These stages are the sensorimotor stage, preoperational stage, concrete operational stage, and formal operational stage. They are described briefly in table 1.1.

Sensorimotor Stage   During Piaget's sensorimotor stage, babies learn through physical interaction with their environments. They begin using mostly reflexes but gradually move toward more and more purposeful behavior. They also begin to use language and to participate in pretend play. Obviously, most homeschooling parents will not be teaching children under three years of age, but the theory would be incomplete without the inclusion of this first stage.

Preoperational Stage   In the next stage, the preoperational stage, children use language quite well, but their thinking is not yet logical. There are several errors listed below that children in this age range quite predictably make. Although children under six or seven years of age make up a fairly small proportion of homeschoolers, being aware of some of these errors could help the parent avoid trying

Table 1.1.   Piaget's Cognitive Developmental Stages

Stage	Ages	Description
Sensorimotor	birth to 2 yrs	Babies learn through moving, watching, touching, and mouthing
Preoperational	2 to 6 yrs	Children's thinking is not yet logical
Concrete operational	6 to 11+ yrs	Children's thinking becomes logical, but they cannot understand abstract concepts
Formal operational	11+ yrs and older	Children can think as sophisticatedly as adults, using abstract reasoning and thinking hypothetically

to force the child to do something that he or she is not yet developmentally able to do. Piaget's terms, some of which he created, are defined as follows:

Conservation. Conservation is the ability to realize that an amount does not change even though its appearance changes. Children in the preoperational stage are not able to conserve. There are several ways that Piaget showed this. The simplest is the conservation of number. First, two rows of objects, such as candy or pennies, are placed directly across from each other; the objects in each row are spaced apart equally. The child is asked whether each row contains the same amount of objects or if one or the other has more.

After the child agrees that both rows contain the same amount, the adult adds more space between the objects in one row and asks the question again. The preoperational child will insist that the longer row contains more. Piaget discussed conservation in several other areas as well. The idea is always the same. The appearance of the substance changes (distance between pennies, liquid poured from one shape of container to another, modeling clay formed into different shapes), but the actual amount does not.

Reversibility. Reversibility is the ability of the child to retrace steps either physically or mentally. Children younger than six or seven years do not have this ability. Therefore, when the preschool-age child is asked, "what happened?" after a household crisis has occurred and the child says, "I don't know," he or she is not necessarily being elusive. It is quite likely that he or she truly cannot retrace the events that precipitated the crisis.

Seriation. Seriation is the ability to order objects from smallest to largest, darkest to lightest, or some other characteristic. Once children learn this, they adore tasks that require it, but most are unable to do such tasks until at least five years old.

Animism. Animism is attributing lifelike qualities to inanimate objects. For example, a child might insist that his or her teddy bear is hungry. It is not clear whether children truly believe these objects are alive or are just not troubled by the fact they are not.

Class Inclusion/Hierarchical Classification. Until school-age children are able to comprehend these tasks, they cannot understand different levels of grouping. A preoperational child might look at a group of three cars and five trucks and answer the question "are there more trucks or more vehicles?" with "more trucks" because they will not spontaneously group the cars and trucks into a larger group.

Centration. Centration has to do with focusing on only one dimension of something while neglecting all other dimensions. To illustrate, take the example of a child who fails to grasp the conservation task of water being moved from a tall, narrow container to a wide container. He or she may fail because of the errant focus only on the height of the water rather than also considering the change in the width of the water.

Egocentricity. Preschool children do not realize that everyone does not see things from their perspective, and therefore, according to Piaget, they are egocentric. A good example of this is when a preschooler seems surprised that another child is mad when the first child takes the second child's toy. The first child wanted it; therefore, doesn't the whole world want him to have it?

Concrete Operational Stage   In the concrete operational stage, children's thinking becomes logical but they are limited to only thinking about things with which they have experience. They will have gained the ability to do all of the tasks that preoperational children cannot do. However, concrete-stage children cannot think hypothetically or abstractly, which means they would have difficulty using and understanding abstract words, such as love, truth, and freedom. They also may struggle with many types of math problems and will have difficulty with hypothesis testing, as is often done in science courses.

Formal Operational Stage   Piaget originally believed that the last stage of cognitive development, formal operational, began around age eleven. However, he later modified that number upward. Most research has shown that there are actually many people, even whole cultures, who do not have the ability to use formal operations. This is the stage in which people gain the ability to understand abstract concepts, to formally test hypotheses, and to think idealistically. Even those who do gain the ability to think formally probably do not do so in all areas. For example, I can think formally about psychology, but I can think only concretely about automobile repair or nuclear physics.

Applications of Piagetian Cognitive Developmental Theory

If Piaget was correct in saying that children progress through stages automatically and that they cannot be sped up, then tasks should be suited to their developmental stage. It would be inappropriate to require eight-year-olds to answer abstract questions or to ask five-year-olds to solve conservation-type problems. Also, if Piaget's notion is true that the best learning occurs through active involvement and exploration, then hands-on opportunities for the child to learn would be preferable to handing a child a completed study sheet to memorize.

VYGOTSKY'S DIALECTICAL THEORY

Vygotsky's (1987) theory, which was developed about the same time as Piaget's, was fairly complicated, but the central ideas are quite simple and quite useful. First, Vygotsky believed that children learn and improve their thinking by internalizing dialogues of wiser people. That is a fancy way to say that children memorize our conversations. Vygotsky believed that children learn to think and improve their ability to think through interacting and talking with other older/wiser people, learning the words that are spoken.

For example, when teaching someone to tie a shoe, the teacher almost always narrates. The child then talks him- or herself through the process using the teacher's words. It goes something like this: "See, you cross this string over, tuck it under, and pull it through, then you make a loop. Now you try it." Then the child tries to tie a shoe and sometime in the process says, "make a loop."

A second very useful concept taught by Vygotsky was called the zone of proximal development (ZPD). Tasks that fall in the ZPD for a particular child are those that are relatively easy to accomplish with a little bit of help but are too difficult to accomplish alone. He called that little bit of help that is given by the older/wiser person *scaffolding*.

Unlike Piaget, Vygotsky did not speak of stages. He saw the development of thinking (cognition) as being closely related to how much help was received and internalized.

Applications of Vygotsky's Dialectical Theory

There are several areas to which Vygotsky's ideas could be applied. First, purposefully carrying on a dialogue with the child or in the child's presence will benefit his or her thinking and learning. To some parents this comes naturally; however, to a quiet parent, this might have to be done more consciously. Second, tutoring from either an adult or even another student can provide that scaffolding that is needed to help the child accomplish something within his or her ZPD.

A seemingly obvious application would be actually teaching a child, not just allowing independent learning, as Piaget would have preferred. Vygotsky would be in favor of actually teaching content as well as problem solving to the students. However, Vygotsky was similar to Piaget in that both were in favor of active learning and hands-on examples, rather than just having complete information handed to the student.

RECEPTIVE LEARNING/EXPOSITORY TEACHING

Receptive learning and expository teaching are two names for the teaching method promoted by David Ausubel (Ausubel, Novak, and Hanesian, 1978). His belief was that the most efficient way to increase the knowledge that students possess would be to directly teach it to them in a meaningful way. He believed that in order to learn, students must file new information within the knowledge they already have. He promoted the idea of organizing knowledge before teaching it, piquing curiosity using "advance organizers," and lecturing. An advance organizer would be an attention-getter that prepares a student to learn the information by reminding him or her of previous learning. It could be an interesting science demonstration or a curiosity-producing question. The gist of his theory was that the student's existing knowledge would be activated, making it easier to learn the new information.

In terms of organization, Ausubel taught that the more organized the information, the easier it should be to learn, whether it is in lecture or written form. This organization could take the form of outlines, section headings, or even transitional phrases such as "the next section we will cover will be . . ." Although a focus of Ausubel's ideas relate to how to lecture effectively—and very few homeschoolers lecture—the same principles could be applied to the process of explaining lessons or conveying expectations in other areas. When boiled down, Ausubel's instructions for lecturing have been taught in many speech classes over the decades: "Tell them what you are going to tell them, tell them what you want them to know, then tell them what you told them." As redundant as this comes across, it has been shown that we learn information much better when it is organized (Bowman, 1979; Schonwetter, 1993).

INFORMATION PROCESSING

Information processing refers to how we remember things. The basic idea of information processing uses a computer as an analogy for how human memory works. Just as a computer has input (keyboard, mouse, telephone line), we have input (ears, eyes, fingers). Just as a computer has storage (hard drive, floppy disk, CD), we have memory (short-term memory, long-term memory). Just as a computer has output (monitor, printer), we have output (voice, writing). There are two main information-processing theories, Atkinson and Shiffrin's (1968) three-store model and Craik and Lockhart's (1972) levels of processing.

Three-Store Model

The three-store model describes memory as having three parts. The first is called the *sensory register* (or sensory registers, one for each sense: one visual, one auditory, one touch, etc.). This is that hypothetical place where information is instantaneously stored as it comes in as a physical sensation. The information is either attended to and sent on for further processing or it is ignored.

For example, a man goes to Cracker Barrel (for those who are unfamiliar with Cracker Barrel, it is a combination restaurant and gift shop found about every forty miles along interstates in the southeastern United States), puts his name on the waiting list, and shops around for ceramic figurines while waiting for a table. When he hears a name called, his sensory register keeps it for a couple of seconds. If it is his name, he will continue to process it by heading for a table. If not, it will disappear almost immediately. If someone were to ask him in a couple of minutes what name had been called, he would most likely not know.

The second storage area is called the *short-term memory* or the *working memory*. Whatever is currently being thought about is stored for several seconds in the short-term memory. If it is rehearsed it can be stored there indefinitely. When a phone number is repeated over and over until it is dialed, it is held in the short-term memory. What was just read in this book was processed in short-term memory.

The third storage area is the *long-term memory*. The long-term memory is where information is permanently stored (or at least is stored for a very long time). The main goal of teaching, studying, and attending school, according to an information-processing theorist, is to have students store information in the long-term memory.

Levels of Processing

The main idea of levels of processing theory developed by Craik and Lockhart (1972) is that information processed at a deep level will be remembered better than information processed at a shallow level.

For example, a teacher requires students to learn the names of the first five presidents. One student is given a list of presidents to memorize and recall on a test. The other student is given an interesting fact about each president and then asked to match each president to that interesting fact. Craik and Lockhart would say the second student would remember the presidents much better because he or she had to "do more" with the information. Research has shown this to be true.

This may explain why it is often said that something is not really known until it has been taught. Teaching material usually takes quite a deep level of processing. Just think what experts homeschooling parents will become, having taught all subjects to all ages.

Applications of Information Processing Theories

If, indeed, information-processing theorists are correct, then how does someone learn (or store) information? The most commonly used method is *rehearsing*. This can come in the form of repeating information aloud or silently over and over. Students could read and reread material or rewrite material as a way to rehearse. Levels of processing theorists would say this is the least efficient method of memorizing. Other tried and tested learning (or memory) techniques that have emerged from the research on information processing are as follows:

Overlearning. This is an extreme type of rehearsal. Information is rehearsed to the point that it is very difficult to forget.

Automaticity. This is practicing something to the point that it is automatic, so no thought processes have to be used. An example is learning to write. When a child first learns to write, he or she has to think about how to make each letter, how each word was spelled, and how to keep the words on the lines. Later concepts can be written without any thought being given to the mechanics of writing.

Grouping. Classifying lists on the basis of common characteristics can aid memory. Remembering the key element of the group is a key to remembering all the items. An example would be grouping animals together as mammals, reptiles, amphibians, or birds.

Rhymes and Songs. Information put into rhyme improves recall, and adding a tune enhances it even more. Most of us learned the alphabet by learning the "ABC" song, which has a tune and rhymes.

Acronyms or Acrostics and Initial Letter Strategies. Acronyms or acrostics can help in remembering lists of words. The first letter from each word in a list forms a key word, such as using the word FACE to stand for the spaces on the treble clef in music. Acronyms are now part of our language. Consider IBM, AT&T, CIA, MGM, USA, and FBI. Also, the first letters of each member of a list can be used to create a sentence; for example, "every good boy does fine" uses the notes on the lines of the treble clef to begin each word of the sentence.

Visual Association. Visual association refers to imagining something or picturing it. In order to aid memory, a visual image can be thought of that will remind the person of the material. The stranger that image is, the more effective the image will be. For example, if a student was trying to remember that the word for duck in Spanish is *pato*, he or she could remember an image of a duck with a pot on its head.

Method of Loci. In using the method of loci (which actually means location), the student visualizes a room or route that is familiar. Items or ideas to be remembered are mentally placed around the room or along the route. This is especially helpful in giving speeches or remembering lists of important points in a correct sequence.

Additional research findings include:

Serial Position Effects. Information at the beginning or the end of a list, a lecture, a magazine article, or any other source of information tends to be remembered better than the information in the middle.

Attention Span. The attention span refers to how long an individual can pay attention to something. This is quite brief for small children (a few seconds or minutes) and gradually increases with age.

Processing Speed. Processing speed refers to how quickly someone is able to process information. It is known that some people process quickly and others process more slowly. Most intelligence tests have some measure of processing speed, but it is not known whether it is actually a component of intelligence or not.

Memory Techniques. Teaching and encouraging the use of memory techniques enhances the amount of material that is remembered.

BEHAVIORAL LEARNING THEORY

B. F. Skinner (1953) popularized behavioral learning theory in the 1950s. Its focus is on changing actual behavior rather than investigating or trying to change the underlying causes of behavior. The use of reinforcement or reward to increase good behaviors and punishment to decrease bad behaviors are the central applications of the theory. Although behaviorism is presented here in the context of learning, it is also easily applied to motivation and discipline as well, and it is discussed in the chapters addressing those topics.

Techniques in Behavioral Learning Theory

There are several very simple processes that are associated with behaviorism. Those are reinforcement, extinction, and punishment.

Reinforcement. Reinforcement occurs when the consequence that follows a behavior makes it more likely that a behavior will occur again. For example, if a child completes his or her work on time and with few errors and the parent is appreciative, the child will be more likely to continue completing work on time.

There are many things that can be reinforcing, including praise, candy, money, special activities, and free time. It is the parent's job to study the child to learn what is reinforcing to that child. Those things that reinforce the child's behavior may also change over time. The child may outgrow a particular activity or item or have so much of it (e.g., eating too much candy) that it is no longer motivating. Therefore, the parent must continue studying the child and monitoring how effectively various reinforcers work.

A special type of reinforcement is called *shaping*. When shaping is used, a complicated behavior is broken down into small parts. In the beginning each part is reinforced. Gradually, a larger and larger section of the behavior has to be performed to receive reinforcement. This is very helpful with younger children or with anyone who is trying to learn something complicated. Schoolwork, housework, *real* work, and line dancing all lend themselves well to shaping.

While reinforcement increases someone's behavior, punishment and extinction are both used to reduce a behavior or to completely get rid of it.

Extinction. Extinction occurs when the reinforcement that has been keeping a behavior going is removed. For example, if a child constantly asks for help on relatively simple math problems and the parent comes to help each time and guides the child all the way through each problem, the child will most likely continue to ask for help. However, if the parent gives minimal help or instructs the child to work longer without offering help, the child will gradually stop asking.

Without the reinforcement, the behavior eventually disappears. This is an extremely effective, nonpainful way to get rid of an unwanted behavior; however, it takes a while, so it should not be used for dangerous behaviors. At times it is also difficult to determine what is reinforcing a behavior, or it is difficult to remove the reinforcer even if it can be found. In those situations extinction will not work and punishment must be used.

Punishment. Punishment involves either doing something negative to a person (a spanking for running out in the street, being sent to jail for driving under the influence of drugs) or removing something positive (losing the privilege of going to a friend's party for being late for curfew) to lessen or stop a behavior. Just as a parent should study the child to learn what is reinforcing to the child, he or she should also determine what is negative to the child. Also, just as reinforcers can lose their ability to reinforce, punishers can lose their ability to punish. A child can get used to spankings, groundings, or whatever punishment has been used.

Schedules of Reinforcement

How reinforcement or punishment is used can greatly affect how well it works (or whether it works at all). The factor that has the most impact on effectiveness is the consistency, or schedule, used with the various techniques.

Continuous. Reinforcing or punishing a behavior every time it occurs is called continuous. This is the *only* schedule that should be used with punishment because anything more intermittent will worsen behavior instead of improving it. It can also be used with reinforcement effectively, but it takes a lot of time, effort, and possibly expense, depending on the reinforcer being used.

Fixed ratio. Fixed-ratio reinforcement involves reinforcing a behavior after a certain number of times it occurs (a jelly bean for every five math problems completed).

Fixed interval. Fixed-interval reinforcement involves reinforcing a behavior on a fixed schedule as long as the behavior is done sometime during the time period (a paycheck every Friday as long as any work has been done during that week).

Variable ratio. Variable-ratio reinforcement involves reinforcing a behavior after a random number of times it is performed (a slot machine).

Variable interval. Variable-interval reinforcement involves reinforcing a behavior after a varying amount of time (a salesman gets occasional commission checks, sometimes after a week, sometimes after two or three).

The most important reason to be aware of schedules of reinforcement is to understand why behavioral learning strategies are or are not working. The ideal way to teach something using behaviorism is to reinforce the desired behavior and then to gradually stretch out either the time between reinforcers or the number of behaviors (perhaps math problems) that must be completed to receive the reinforcer. The hope is that the desired behavior will become a habit and the parent will not have to reinforce it anymore. Punishment is a different case. To remove a behavior, it should be punished absolutely every time it occurs, if there is any way possible. This convinces the child that there is no reason to do the behavior because it will always result in punishment. If someone is allowed to get away with a behavior that has been declared wrong, it actually serves as a variable schedule of reinforcement, increasing the likelihood that it will continue.

Other Factors Affecting the Effectiveness of Behavioral Techniques

The factors that have the most impact on the effectiveness of behavioral learning techniques are consistency and immediacy. Generalization and discrimination are also important when teaching the child in what contexts a behavior is expected or appropriate.

Consistency. The more consistent the punishment, reinforcement, and extinction, the more effective they will be. What this consistency does is convince the child that the parent means what is said. This breeds trust between the parent and the child, which goes much further than simply controlling behavior.

Immediacy. The more immediate the consequence of a behavior occurs, the more effective it will be. If a reinforcer or punisher is delayed, it is less likely to be associated with the behavior and is less likely to change that behavior in the future.

Generalization. It would be inefficient to try to teach a child every behavior in every setting. What is preferred is for the child to use what has been learned through reinforcement and punishment in one setting and apply it to new situations in which it is appropriate. An example is a child who has learned to multiply fractions in his math curriculum and can use that knowledge to figure the server's tip in a restaurant.

Discrimination. The opposite of generalization is discrimination. Sometimes there are certain behaviors that are appropriate in one context but not another. It may be appropriate to look through a textbook to find answers when working on seatwork or study questions, but it is unacceptable during a test. It is valuable to be able to discriminate (or distinguish) between situations that get reinforced or punished and those that do not.

Maintenance (Fading)

No parent or teacher wants to have to go around reinforcing or punishing children or students all the time, and therefore they must be weaned from both. By gradually fading reinforcement, the children get into the habit of doing whatever the behavior is with less and less reinforcement. Eventually none is needed. As mentioned earlier, the same thing will not work with punishment. Every single time the inappropriate behavior occurs, it should be punished. However, if the same punishment is being used and the behavior continues, the punishment is not working and should be changed.

MODELING AND IMITATION

Much learning actually comes from watching what other people do and what happens to them afterward. People, children included, tend to imitate those things that work out well and avoid imitating those things that do not turn out well for others. Therefore, a practical teaching strategy would be to model the behavior that is expected from the children, in both academic and nonacademic areas.

SUMMARY OF LEARNING THEORIES

It is apparent that there are many diverse views of how people learn. Material included in this chapter illustrates concepts that have been supported by research studies over the years. None actually conflict, but they do not fit neatly together, either. The most useful application of this information is probably to pick and choose concepts or strategies that explain or assist in a child's learning.

2

ACADEMIC ABILITY

Academic ability, as defined here, includes both intelligence and prior learning. Intelligence relates more to people's capacity to learn, how naturally things come to them, or how quickly they learn. Prior learning is what they already know, which they have acquired through experience, schooling, or some other means.

The ability of students *and their homeschooling parents* is important to discuss because this will influence several aspects of homeschooling. The student's level of intelligence will determine the difficulty of materials to be used, the speed with which material is covered, and the parental expectations, at least to some extent. The student's prior learning will have an impact on what the student is ready to learn, or in other words, where the parent should begin.

The student's intelligence and prior learning are only parts of the equation, however. The parent or parents who will be responsible for the child's education also have a certain level of intelligence and a certain amount of prior learning. A parent with a great deal of education or who is very intelligent may have more options when it comes to teaching his or her children than a parent with limited education or a more modest level of intelligence. This does not mean that the latter should not homeschool. It just means that more structured material will have to be used. This became very apparent to me as I taught my son calculus after my own experience of taking one semester of the subject more than twenty years earlier. That is why answer books and solutions manuals are made. How difficult it would have been if I had been required to make up all of the problems and solutions. Luckily, someone more experienced in calculus had done that for me.

INTELLIGENCE

What is intelligence? That debate has raged for thousands of years. There are theorists who have claimed it is one entity: at birth a person gets the amount he or she gets, and that is all (Spearman, 1904). I like to describe his theory with the analogy of a bucket. Everyone is born with an *intelligence bucket*. When our bucket is filled, some have a full bucket, some have a partially filled bucket, and some have just a drop in the bucket. If one believes that idea, there would be little reason to try to boost low intelligence, and there could be no credit taken for high intelligence. However, there are many competing views. Some believe that intelligence is made up of two (Cattell, 1963; Horn, 1994; Horn and Cattell, 1967), three (Sternberg, 1988; 1990), eight (Gardner, 1993a; 1993b), or even 150 (Guilford, 1967; Meeker, 1969) different components.

Theories of Intelligence

As mentioned, there are several theories about what constitutes intelligence. All do not have equal research support. Gardner's theory is the least well defended from a research standpoint but probably the most popular at the moment. There are some interesting activities based on his theory; however, the rationale behind the theory may not be sound.

There are also people who don't even believe in intelligence as a characteristic (or at least they don't think it should be measured or considered in decision making). This idea seems to come from the perspective of not comparing or making anyone who is comparatively less intelligent feel bad. We do know that people do achieve different scores on IQ tests, and those who score lower tend to need more assistance with educational activities, and those who score higher tend to need less help. A good rule of thumb may be to consider that IQ testing can be a good place to begin to plan for educational experiences but not a reason to place someone in a pigeonhole from which they cannot escape.

Spearman Spearman (1904), mentioned in the previous bucket analogy, thought that intelligence is inborn and that each person has a fixed amount. He called it *g* for general intelligence. This was the prevalent belief about intelligence for quite a long time. Later theories appeared that broke intelligence into different areas.

Cattell and Horn Cattell and Horn (Cattell, 1963; Horn, 1994; Horn and Cattell, 1967) saw intelligence as made up of two areas of ability, although they are very highly correlated with each other and may just be different aspects of the same thing—general intelligence. They called these two components *fluid* and *crystallized intelligence*.

Fluid intelligence is the ability to solve new problems and basically to think on one's feet. Scores on tests of fluid intelligence tend to decline somewhat with age unless the mind is kept active.

Crystallized intelligence is often described as book learning. It is the ability to accumulate knowledge such as word definitions, historical facts, and social customs. Usually, scores on tests of crystallized intelligence gradually increase with age. People get old and wise and tell stories about "ancient" childhoods.

Sternberg Sternberg's (Sternberg, 1988; 1990) triarchic theory of intelligence speaks of intelligence as having three components: 1) componential, which includes what is typically thought of as intelligence, such as accumulating knowledge; 2) experiential, which has to do with the ability to learn from experience; and 3) contextual, which has to do with functioning within a particular context, in other words, street smarts.

Guilford Guilford's structure of intellect (SI) theory contains the most components of any of the well-known, published theories of intelligence—150 (Guilford, 1967; Meeker, 1969). Obviously, with this many various components, there is no way the components could be addressed individually, either in intelligence testing or through teaching applications. His theory is mentioned here just to demonstrate the extreme variability of the prevailing ideas of intelligence.

Gardner   Currently, Gardner's (Gardner, 1993a; 1993b) theory of multiple intelligences is probably the most popular in educational circles. He believes, as several of the other theorists mentioned, that we actually have intelligence in several areas. However, his components probably deviate more than any other well-known theory from what is typically associated with intelligence. He includes traditional areas, such as verbal and mathematical ability, but also areas such as intrapersonal intelligence, which relates to knowing oneself well, and naturalist intelligence, which relates to appreciating seasonal changes and activities such as hiking. The areas he identified are:

Verbal/Linguistic: learning and understanding language/words

Mathematical/Logical: having mathematical, logical, analytical ability

Musical: liking and performing music

Visuo Spatial: understanding dimension, directions, and drawing well

Kinesthetic: having athletic ability, coordination

Interpersonal: understanding and getting along with others

Intrapersonal: understanding and getting along with oneself

Naturalist: enjoying nature, hiking, appreciating seasonal changes (this one is newer than the others; there used to be just seven)

Teachers have taken Gardner's ideas and run with them, although classroom application was not his original intent. It seems to be very appealing to be able to find some area of giftedness for every child. There are online instruments to determine intelligence as defined by Gardner and myriad activities to capitalize on areas of strength and weakness. Although there is popular support for Gardner's theory, there is not much research support for either his components of intelligence or the academic applications of his theory.

Obviously there are many views of intelligence. Typically, problem solving, verbal ability, and mathematic ability are included, yet additional components vary greatly.

Heredity or Environment?

There is also debate about whether intelligence is innate or due to environmental influences—or both. Estimates have been given from "almost totally inherited" to "almost totally environmental." The view that it is mostly inherited would make it seem futile to try to influence someone's intelligence. The view that it is almost entirely environmentally influenced would create a great deal of pressure to provide the very best environment and many types of intelligence-boosting opportunities.

OK, So What Is Intelligence?

For the sake of argument, we will just assume there is something, whether it is called intelligence or not, that makes learning easier for some people and more difficult for others. All of the following definitions for this "something" have been used at one point or another:

Score on an IQ test
General potential for learning
Several specific areas of learning potential
Information processing speed

How Is Intelligence Measured?

This is not a psychological testing book, so the descriptions will be brief. There are a multitude of ways that intelligence has been measured, including answering questions on paper with a pencil and fitting the last piece in a puzzle. In public and private schools, a paper–pencil test is generally administered, with an annual standardized achievement tests. They are used to screen children. If a child receives a score at the high end (usually around 130 or higher) or the low end (usually around 70 or lower), the child is referred for individual testing to determine whether he or she qualifies for special education services. Generally, above 130 is considered gifted and below 70 is considered mentally handicapped.

An individually administered IQ test is given by a trained testing professional to one individual child. The test will typically include definitions, puzzles, cartoons, blocks, numbers, and various other tasks. Some school systems may be willing to provide intelligence testing for homeschooled students, but this would likely vary from school system to school system. If testing is not available through the school system, having a child's intelligence tested by a psychologist or other qualified person can cost several hundred dollars. There are some fairly good online IQ tests that can be used to get an idea of an older child's intelligence—and also that of the parent(s). Typing "IQ tests" into any Internet search engine, such as Google or Yahoo, will result in several choices of IQ tests.

Can IQ Be Changed?

It is important not only to have an idea of the intelligence of the child and the parent, but also to know whether IQ can be changed. The answer is that it can, to some extent. It is most likely that someone with an IQ of 80 will never have an IQ of 120, but he or she very likely may reach 95 (actually a pretty big jump). Environmental enrichment or impoverishment seems to affect IQ over long periods of time. Studies have shown that over a period of many years (ten or twelve), the IQs of children in enriched environments (lots of books, reading, educational experiences, and problem-solving opportunities) gradually and steadily rose. The IQs of children in impoverished environments (few books, little conversation, uneducated family members, and few educational experiences) steadily declined over that same period.

If IQ changes over time due to just the type of environment in which the child is reared, do interventions specifically targeting IQ increases work? Programs like Head Start have shown increases in IQ scores if intervention is continued for participating children; however, if it is not continued, these improvements seem to wash out in a couple of years. The implication of these findings reinforces what is believed by many homeschooling parents: the child will benefit most by long-lasting, enriching, challenging, caring instruction.

PRIOR LEARNING

Prior learning relates to what the child (and parent) already knows. The most obvious source of prior learning is previous schooling. However, other sources include experiences such as vacations, trips to museums, television shows, and conversations with more knowledgeable children and adults. It is irrelevant how the child (or parent) learned something. That knowledge should still be taken into consideration when planning where to begin teaching.

IMPLICATIONS OF INTELLIGENCE AND PRIOR LEARNING FOR HOMESCHOOLING

Implications of the Parent's Intelligence

A parent with high intelligence will be able to understand the work that the child is doing, will be able to help the child when he or she finds the material difficult, and will probably be more confident about the teaching process. A parent with lower intelligence will have more difficulty and will probably be less confident. This does not mean that only geniuses should homeschool. It just means that understanding where potential weaknesses lie, and accommodating for those ahead of time, may make the homeschooling experience more pleasant.

Implications of the Child's Intelligence

A highly intelligent child will be able to cover material quickly, may need little help, and will most likely proceed to eventually take more advanced subjects (calculus, chemistry). A child who has lower intelligence, on the other hand, will cover material more slowly and may need more help, possibly much more help.

Implications of the Relationship between a Parent's and a Child's Intelligence

If there is a discrepancy between the parent's and child's intelligence, there could be potential for conflict. Knowing this up front may help to offset some of that conflict. A highly intelligent parent may hold unrealistic expectations for his or her child. Conversely, the parent of a highly intelligent child may have trouble keeping up and keeping him or her challenged.

Testing If Necessary

If it is suspected that a child is functioning above or below where he or she should be, it might be beneficial to have him or her tested (not just IQ, but achievement as well). This can help determine if he or she is struggling in specific areas or if he or she is probably doing the best he or she can be expected to do. It also may help to pinpoint areas of strength that could be enhanced.

Appropriate Schoolwork

Students should have schoolwork that is appropriately difficult but doable. The ability to tailor the level of the work to the student is one of the primary benefits of homeschooling. The goal should not be to ensure a student is working at exactly the same level as other children at the same grade or age, but to have him or her challenged appropriately. If material is too far beyond his or her ability, he or she will not learn it and will become frustrated. If it is too easy, he or she will learn far less than possible and will get bored. A challenge seems to be best.

Appropriate Expectations

Having an understanding of a child's overall intelligence level and the speed at which he or she works can help the teacher or parent have appropriate expectations. This is not to say "let them off; they are slow" or "don't challenge them; they aren't very bright" but to have a reasonable idea of what to expect. It should be remembered, though, that students really do rise to the expectations placed on them, but those expectations need to be attainable.

Intervention Where Needed

Sometimes, for a child who has extreme deficits or extreme areas of giftedness, extra help may be needed. That could come in the form of consultation with someone who has worked with similar children, finding Web sites with helpful ideas, or studying to become acquainted with possible interventions.

PERSONALITY

Some personalities seem to be better suited for homeschooling than others. This chapter describes personality characteristics and suggests diagnostic tools for discovering the personality characteristics of parents and children. While there is little research on personality characteristics of homeschoolers, there is a great deal of research on the subject in general. These characteristics are discussed as they relate to decisions of whether or not to homeschool and what types of instruction, discipline, and motivational techniques to use.

There are many ways to define personality. The aspects of personality dealt with in this chapter are temperament and learning style. The reason these aspects were chosen was that they are fairly tangible and have been investigated in many research studies.

Just as in dealing with varying opinions regarding intelligence, there is disagreement as to whether there are innate differences in temperament or learning style. Some say that all people are alike, and others say people have innate differences that must be catered to. Many people fall somewhere in between. These characteristics may be just preferences or virtually unchangeable characteristics. Whichever they are, it may be helpful to attempt to develop the most beneficial traits and to use, or at least take into consideration, the natural inclinations of the child (and parent) when planning and teaching.

TEMPERAMENT

Certain combinations of temperaments among homeschooling parents and their children can result in schooling that goes smoothly. Other mixtures can be quite frustrating for the parents and the children.

Thomas and Chess Dimensions of Temperament

One of the oldest and most widely used classifications of temperament was developed in the 1950s by Thomas and Chess, who followed a group of children over many years, looking at behavioral styles (Thomas and Chess, 1977). Their descriptions of temperament characteristics included mood quality (e.g., happy vs. sad), schedule orientation (e.g., highly scheduled vs. unscheduled), and intensity of reactions (e.g., very reactive vs. passive). Combinations of these characteristics resulted in their identifying three temperament clusters. These clusters were labeled as *easy*, *difficult*, and *slow-to-warm-up*. The *easy* child is rhythmic, follows a schedule easily, is typically pleasant, and is flexible when faced with change. The largest proportion of children falls in this category (approximately 40 percent). The *difficult* child is just the opposite. He or she is less predictable, does not respond well to change, and has frequent negative reactions. It is estimated that about 10 percent of children fall in this category. The *slow-to-warm-up* child generally responds with low intensity and takes a long time to become accustomed to new people and new situations. Approximately 15 percent of children are thought to be slow-to-warm-up. The remaining children are believed to be some mixture of these temperament types.

Hippocratic Temperaments

A second classification of temperaments, the Hippocratic temperaments, dates from ancient times (Childs, 1995). Repopularized by authors such as LaHaye (1984), the temperaments are labeled as *sanguine*, *choleric*, *phlegmatic*, and *melancholic*. These will be described in detail, but before reading those descriptions, the instrument shown in figure 3.1 can be completed.

Figure 3.1. Personality Assessment Sheet (adapted from personality descriptions originated by Galen and Hippocrates; for an example, see Childs, 1995; and LaHaye, 1984)

Circle the traits that are descriptive of you. Subtotal the strengths and weaknesses. Add these subtotals to determine the grand total for each personality type. The highest numbers indicate your personality type.

Strengths

animated	adventurous	analytical	adaptable
playful	persuasive	persistent	peaceful
sociable	self-sacrificing	strong-willed	submissive
convincing	competitive	considerate	controlled
refreshing	resourceful	respectful	reserved
spirited	self-reliant	sensitive	satisfied
promoter	positive	planner	patient
spontaneous	sure	scheduled	shy
optimistic	outspoken	orderly	obliging
funny	forceful	faithful	friendly
delightful	daring	detailed	diplomatic
cheerful	confident	cultured	consistent
inspiring	independent	idealistic	inoffensive
demonstrative	decisive	deep	dry humor
mixes easily	mover	musical	mediator
talker	tenacious	thoughtful	tolerant
lively	leader	loyal	listener
cute	chief	chart maker	contented
popular	productive	perfectionist	pleasant
bouncy	bold	behaved	balanced

| Sanguine | Choleric | Melancholy | Phlegmatic |

Weaknesses

brassy	bossy	bashful	blank
undisciplined	unsympathetic	unforgiving	unenthusiastic
repetitious	resistant	resentful	reticent
forgetful	frank	fussy	fearful
interrupts	impatient	insecure	indecisive
unpredictable	unaffectionate	unpopular	uninvolved
haphazard	headstrong	hard to please	hesitant
permissive	proud	pessimistic	plain
angered easily	argumentative	alienated	aimless
naïve	nervy	negative attitude	nonchalant
wants credit	workaholic	withdrawn	worrier
talkative	tactless	too sensitive	timid
disorganized	domineering	depressed	doubtful
inconsistent	intolerant	introvert	indifferent
messy	manipulative	moody	mumbles
show-off	stubborn	skeptical	slow
loud	lord over others	loner	lazy
scatterbrained	short tempered	suspicious	sluggish
restless	rash	revengeful	reluctant
changeable	crafty	critical	compromising

| Sanguine | Choleric | Melancholy | Phlegmatic |

Totals

| Sanguine | Choleric | Melancholy | Phlegmatic |

Cholerics. Cholerics are driven, task-oriented doers. They may cut corners and bend rules, and they have to go it alone because they take risks and are always looking for a better way. They desire to make a difference and to be in the action. Of course, although they are natural leaders, they tend to be very impatient and do not naturally possess strong people skills, which may impede their ability to work in teams. But, if they are motivated for the task, it will get done. They are very responsible that way.

Sanguines. Sanguines are gregarious partiers. They enjoy being in groups, forming groups, and leading groups. Sanguines are bored by day-to-day tasks and are not bridled by the need to be neat or organized. They don't take themselves or any task too seriously, don't worry about making mistakes, and tend to be creative and able to befriend and motivate large numbers of people. Some of the weaknesses of sanguines include being late and becoming annoyed with other personality types who take themselves and their tasks much more seriously.

Phlegmatics. Phlegmatics are the steady, trustworthy, unemotional friends. They avoid conflict and don't rush to complete tasks. They just plod along. The primary weakness with phlegmatics is that they may be stubborn. They aren't looking for a new experience and really don't want to have one.

Melancholies. Melancholies tend to be hesitant worriers. They usually want to be perfect and don't want to get too close to anyone because the person might find out that they aren't perfect.

Sometimes personality instruments seem too simplified. Most of us are mixtures of personality characteristics. However, coming to realize some characteristics of the child to be homeschooled and the parent who will be doing the homeschooling can reduce some tension. This does not mean that there will not be conflict or that everyone will agree all the time, but perhaps playing up the strengths and downplaying the weaknesses of the personality type of each party can head off some of the conflict. There are additional personality-test resources included in the appendix.

LEARNING STYLES

Much has been said about learning styles in recent years, and much of it conflicts. This section of this chapter will give an overview of learning styles and how these might relate to the process of homeschooling. After becoming familiar with learning styles, the difficulty arises when one tries to decide how to use the information. Should the student be allowed or encouraged to use the style he or she is most comfortable with? Should emphasis be placed on developing those that he or she is less comfortable with? Should he or she have to use all of them? There is not enough research evidence to make a determination. Therefore, the information is given, and it is up to the judgment of the reader as to how to apply it.

This first category of learning styles has to do with what sensory mechanism is most often used or best used when learning. All people use all of them, but some people seem to prefer one, and others prefer another. These are visual, auditory, and kinesthetic learning styles.

Visual

Visual learners learn best by reading or seeing the information. Pictures are helpful, as are charts, graphs, and diagrams.

Auditory

Auditory learners learn best by hearing. Lectures, recordings, videotapes, and quizzing aloud are helpful.

Kinesthetic

Kinesthetic learners learn best through hands-on experience. Touching, feeling, and actually trying something for themselves helps them learn best.

The next grouping of learning styles has to do with the degree to which a child relies on context in his or her learning. Some are said to be field dependent and others are said to be field independent.

Field Dependent

Field-dependent learners see things in context and need the context to understand things. Usually, people who are field dependent prefer to work in groups and have social interaction. The implication of this is that students might like to ask questions, talk, and possibly be in the room with someone as they work on their schoolwork. The ability to bounce ideas off someone else could enhance their learning or at least their enjoyment as they learn.

Field Independent

Field-independent learners are analytical. They see things with or without the context and prefer to (or are able to) work alone. The implication of this is that they may prefer to work at their own pace and probably would prefer little conversation or interaction during learning time.

The final grouping of learning styles has to do with the way tasks are approached. Rather than two discrete groups, it is actually a continuum from reflective to impulsive.

Impulsive

Impulsive learners tend to act before they think, hurry through assignments, jump at the first reasonable answer on a test, and try to take shortcuts. Obviously, this can be detrimental to performance. Their grades may not reflect their understanding of material because they have not taken time to carefully consider questions. While a degree of impulsivity may be beneficial on a timed test, usually it is more harmful than helpful.

A way to reduce impulsivity is to increase the child's reflectivity by teaching him or her to practice talking through the steps that should be taken when problem solving. For example, if a student rushes through her math, she can be instructed to sit and write out each step while narrating what is being done, step by step. Gradually, the steps can be written without saying them aloud. After practicing this many times, she will be more likely to slow down a bit to go through each step.

Reflective

Reflective learners think so much they may never act. They tend to think things out, sometimes quite slowly and deliberately. They want to make sure they have covered all of their bases and looked at every possible angle. This can hurt their work and keep them from being able to finish by causing them to second-guess themselves and change answers. While reflectivity is probably more conducive to academic success than is impulsivity, somewhere in the middle is best.

APPLICATION OF LEARNING STYLES INFORMATION

Although there is little definitive research on the effects of accommodating learning styles, it seems to make intuitive sense to provide schoolwork that uses multiple senses. This way, whichever strengths children have will probably be tapped. They also will be presented with material that requires the use of their weaker areas and may strengthen those. Some lessons can be presented more visually, some more auditorily, and a few hands-on. The problem with too many hands-on activities is that they tend to be more time-consuming.

4

CHOOSING CURRICULUM

As mentioned previously, there are many decisions that must be made when choosing curriculum. These include assessment of the personalities and abilities involved, but they also depend heavily on the parents' philosophies of what school should and should not include and how material should be taught. The chapter on learning theories may have helped to clarify what the parent believes to be effective ways to teach material. Format, content, amount of coverage, and cost are important considerations when choosing curriculum and are covered in this chapter.

FORMAT

There are many formats that can be used when homeschooling, from un-schooling, which is very unstructured and looks very little like traditional school, to a traditional format that is almost undistinguishable from public school other than the location. Much of the decision about what format to use for homeschooling has to do with how much actual time a parent plans to spend in direct teaching activities. This could fall anywhere along a continuum from direct instruction (the most time in direct teaching activities) to self-study (the least amount of time in direct teaching activities).

Direct Instruction

Direct instruction is the type of instruction in which the parent (or teacher) directly explains the material to the child. He or she may go over workbook pages with the child, work examples on the board or paper, and stay with or near the child as his or her work is completed. This format is quite necessary for very young children just starting out. Obviously, if a child cannot read yet, then self-study will be limited. There is more flexibility with older children. Much depends on the personalities of the child and the parent. If the child has a very hard time staying on task, more direct instruction may be required. If the child is fairly obedient and organized, more self-study can be used. Some parents want to be very involved with their children's learning or simply enjoy teaching. Those parents will do more instruction. Others prefer to only intervene when the child struggles. The ability level of the child at any age is also a factor. If the child has a lower level of ability, the parent will most likely have to do more instruction than if the child has a high level of ability.

Self-Study

As stated above, older children, more capable children, and more motivated and organized children may be allowed to do a great deal of self-study. Our children did not begin homeschooling until they were in fifth and seventh grades. They have been quite capable of completing most of their work on their own. We have bought textbooks and curriculum materials that work well for this. Our initial reasoning was that we had a three-month-old baby when we began (who is now six years old). We have since added another child, who is now three years old, and the two take up even more time than the three-month-old did at first. This only confirmed our decision to use mostly self-study or modified self-study materials. We have chosen to give our children their assignments at the beginning of each day, intervening only when they have difficulty. This is also quite helpful when teaching multiple children on multiple levels. To use direct instruction with even just two children would take approximately eight hours per day. If direct instruction were used exclusively, an additional problem would be that there would be little for one child to do as the parent was instructing the other child.

The amount of instruction required is not the only factor that determines what curriculum format to use, but also whether parents value a traditional education program, and if so, how traditional. Some parents want to cover material in a very conventional way, as is typically done in public school. Others want to try something more out of the ordinary. The curriculum formats below have been described in terms of their main characteristics and also the amount of preparation and instruction required of the parent.

Textbook Based

Textbook based is most similar to traditional public school instruction. Textbooks, workbooks, worksheets, and tests are used. Lesson plans, schedules, and prewritten tests are often included as supplements that can be purchased with the textbooks. These supplements have the potential to reduce the amount of preparation time the parent has to commit.

Literature Based

When using literature-based curriculum, rather than using traditional textbooks, subjects are taught from literature (e.g., novels, biographies). Generally, more time is required for preparation because whoever teaches must be familiar with the literature and typically must develop some or all of the evaluations (i.e., tests, quizzes). The thought behind the method is that children are exposed to literature and are more naturally interested in stories than in textbook-style writing.

Children taught with this method probably learn a similar quantity of information if the literature is well chosen; however, it may not translate as easily to measurement on standardized tests.

Computerized

When using computerized instruction, subjects are taught through the use of computer software, which includes reading material, instructional videos, mini-lectures, quizzes, testing, and grading. Many students find this to be quite fun, as games and videos are incorporated to make the material more entertaining. Very little preparation time is required from the parent once the program is set up on a computer. Occasionally, written work must be hand-graded. A drawback of the self-study nature of these programs is that the parent may have little or no idea of what the child is currently studying, which requires some catch-up on the part of the parent if the child needs help. However, a positive outcome is that as the parent grades work using the teacher guides, he or she may also learn or relearn the material.

Video and Satellite

Both video and satellite school typically involve having students watch a classroom instructor teaching in front of an actual class, and therefore they are the types of homeschooling most similar to a traditional classroom. The classes are either videotaped or broadcast over satellite, and most use traditional textbooks. The actual videotaped classroom determines the time spent on a particular topic. The parent is responsible for administering tests and papers and usually does the grading; however, most parents do not view the videotapes with the children. Similar to computer school, this method could also result in parents who have little idea about what the child is currently studying.

Un-Schooling

Probably the most controversial type of homeschooling is what has come to be known as un-schooling. This approach typically does not make use of textbooks and tests, but rather *real-life* experiences from which the child is expected to accumulate an understanding of the world. This could take any amount of preparation time depending on the extent to which the parent orchestrates the activities to produce particular types of learning. However, the parent could do no planning and no evaluation, which would take very little preparation time. The risk of un-schooling is that it is very difficult to determine whether learning has occurred.

CONTENT

There is a great deal of freedom in determining content when home-schooling. In most states there is a vast amount of flexibility until high school. At that point, there are probably some required subjects, but the order in which they are taught and how they are taught is still up to the parent's discretion. How does one choose?

Traditional

Most families choose a fairly traditional curriculum, including math, reading, language, spelling, history, science, and sometimes Bible studies. Physical education is not generally required until high school, but it is beneficial. Our children participated in tae kwon do for that purpose, but swimming, baseball, or playing in the yard could be used as well. Additional activities used either formally or informally could be music, art, sign language, woodshop, or computer science. When a child reaches high school level, he or she probably needs some diverse electives, and fine arts and foreign languages may be required for graduation and are usually required for college admission. The traditional curriculum is preferable if the child is likely to return to public or private school or if achievement as measured by standardized test scores is valued.

If a parent is interested in determining what subjects are typically taught at various ages, there are several sources of information. Most reputable textbook and curriculum companies will publish what is called a *scope and sequence* that tells what is taught in their curriculum and in what order at each grade level. Local school systems also can provide information about what is taught locally at each grade level. For kindergarten through eighth grade, an organization called the Core Knowledge Foundation has published a "detailed outline of specific knowledge to be taught in grades K–8 in Language Arts, American and World History, Geography, Visual Arts, Music, Math, and Science" (Core Knowledge Foundation, 2003).

Nontraditional

Some people choose to homeschool to escape the traditional. Although un-schooling was mentioned previously as an approach to homeschooling, it also bears mentioning with regard to content. Un-schooling families choose to let their children learn just by living life with lots of experiences. They travel, read, garden, and so forth. The idea is that the child will absorb knowledge through experiences. To reiterate, standardized tests would not necessarily be a good measure of the effectiveness of this method. It would also be difficult to rein-tegrate an un-schooled child into public school.

Obviously, there is no requirement to teach from a purely traditional or a purely nontraditional perspective. They can be combined into a modified traditional curriculum in which life experiences are used to meet particular objectives, and textbooks may or may not be used. A prime example was when we took a four-day field trip to New Mexico early in our homeschooling. Although we have always used traditional curriculum, the children, ages ten and thirteen at that time, were as-signed preparatory work for that trip, such as looking up potential tourist attractions and educational sites and figuring schedules. We vis-ited museums, ruins, and Indian reservations, and our children learned budgeting, map reading, and swam for fitness at the hotel.

AMOUNT OF MATERIAL

How much material should be covered? Even classroom teachers strug-gle with this question. If fairly traditional textbooks are used, it is typi-cal to cover approximately one book per year in most subjects. Publish-ers have usually determined how much material can be reasonably covered in a school year. However, most of the powers that be that over-see homeschooling do not check the amount of material covered. Time is the main consideration for public school systems and most home-schooling umbrella organizations, which some states allow to oversee homeschoolers. A typical time requirement is four hours each day for 180 days, or the equivalent. This can be made up of 90 eight-hour days or 360 two-hour days. This amount of time, used efficiently, allows for several subjects to be covered and still allows for some field trips, such as the trip to New Mexico.

Often, public school teachers are not able to complete textbooks during the course of a school year. This means the children were not taught the material at the end of the book. This can become a problem if the next year's textbook assumes that the material was covered. This is one of the great advantages of homeschooling. Whether the material is finished during the current school year or completed at the beginning of the following school year, a homeschooling parent can ensure there are no gaps in the material covered. However, the ultimate amount of material to be covered will be determined by the extent to which quality and quantity are valued. By quality, it is meant that material can be covered very thoroughly until the child's understanding can be verified, and by quantity, it is meant that a large amount of material can be covered.

Quality

One of the great benefits of homeschooling is that material can be covered very thoroughly and enough time can be spent to ensure that the students understand the material. In public schools and many private schools, material is covered, but often only a few students actually master the material. An added benefit of homeschooling is the freedom to encourage mastery. Students can be made to repeat material, correct and retake tests, and study longer in order to master material because there is not an entire classroom of other children ready to go on. The extra time spent on the difficult concepts can reduce the child's feelings of frustration. However, if too much time is spent on very many things, it will reduce the amount of material covered. This can be a problem when it comes to standardized testing because the material on the test may not have been covered, or if the student returns to public or private school he or she may be behind. It is possible that he or she will know the material that has been covered far better than the other children, but may not know as many things.

Quantity

An added benefit of homeschooling is having the opportunity to cover material very rapidly (quantity). One of the most common complaints heard from parents of bright students in public school is that their children are bored and could cover far more material. Homeschoolers have that option. Some will double up and do two years of work in one. The risk of this rapid coverage is just the opposite of the previous problem. The student may have covered lots of material, but he or she may not understand it well and may forget it quickly. Also, if the child returns to public or private school, he or she may be bored because of the necessity of covering material again.

In our years of homeschooling we have attempted to cover material as rapidly as we can while our children maintain high Bs to As on all of their tests. If they slip below that, we review or slow down. We have them correct tests and sometimes quiz questions. This is an added encouragement to be careful as they take tests because they see the additional work as unpleasant. If they study well and test carefully, that work is avoided.

Complete Curriculum or Not?

Many curriculum materials come completely prepared with lesson plans (what the child should cover each day, how many days per week), quizzes, tests, worksheets, and possibly other materials. Probably the most complete, as I have defined it here, are computerized programs. The student reads; completes activities, quizzes, and tests; and receives grades, all on the computer. At the other end of the spectrum would be the un-schoolers who use no curriculum at all.

The benefits of a complete set of curriculum materials are that subjects will be covered in a similar way, which makes for smoother transitions during the school day, and that buying complete curriculum usually is less expensive than buying materials for individual subjects. Some homeschooling parents prefer to choose different subjects from different publishers or to develop their own materials. This offers more flexibility but tends to be more expensive. In our homeschooling experience, we have taught math using only Saxon Math (see, for example, Saxon, 2001; Saxon and Wang, 2002), but we have used computerized curriculum for most other subjects (see for example Alpha Omega Publications, 2003).

However, there are traditional homeschool curriculum materials that take more effort on the part of the parent than the computerized packages, but they also give the parent more control. Some of these have a fairly prescribed order and speed of coverage, but the parent either chooses test questions from a test bank or from the child's reading material. Others rely on less structured instructional material (studying history through reading historical fiction rather than a history textbook). The child may learn as much history, but in order to evaluate that learning the parent would have to be familiar with that piece of historical fiction and be able to test or orally quiz the child to determine whether learning had taken place. The testing chapter covers more thoroughly some of the pros and cons of testing issues.

COST

Cost is a factor in the decision to homeschool and to determine what curriculum to use. If one has been accustomed to paying private school tuition, purchasing homeschooling materials will probably come as a relief, but if a child has been in public school, they may seem more like a weighty investment. After purchasing curriculum for the last three years, our average per-student expenditure has been $200–$300. Of course, one could spend less or far more.

PARENTAL PERSONALITY

After having a chance to do some personality diagnoses, readers should have a good idea of some of the strengths and weaknesses that might have an impact on their effectiveness in homeschooling. If someone tends to be disorganized, a thoroughly organized curriculum would be helpful. If math is an area of weakness, a curriculum that does the math teaching would be best (for example, a computerized curriculum). If a parent knows a lot about a particular subject, direct instruction in that particular subject might be used. Probably the best way to choose curriculum, after having looked at all of these variables, is to talk with people who have used them, make your best guess, and bite the bullet and try some. We have changed at least some of our curriculum materials each of the years we have homeschooled.

One great benefit of homeschooling is that if material for one or even more subjects is not working, there is nothing wrong with changing to other material in the middle of the year (or even earlier). It does cost more, but changing can alleviate frustration and also increase the amount of learning experienced by the student. This is a great benefit homeschoolers have over public and even private schools. Even if curriculum materials are not working in a classroom, it is unlikely that a school would be able to change during the school year.

MOTIVATION

In this chapter, the main theories of motivation that are taught to teacher-education students are covered in layman's terms. For each theory, applications are given and effectiveness is evaluated based on the results of decades of research. Some applications specifically apply to homeschoolers, but the ideas discussed here are applicable to most people in most settings.

In talking about motivating children or students, the parent's or teacher's motivation has to be examined as well. It's difficult for a child to see someone lying on the couch watching television, hear the person tell him, "you ought to go outside and *do* something," and be truly motivated to go outside. So, in reading, everyone's motivation should be kept in mind.

THEORIES OF MOTIVATION

The main theories of motivation are listed below and will be covered in that order.

- Maslow's Need Theory
- Murray's Need Theory

- Achievement Motivation Theory
- Attribution Theory
- Piaget's Disequilibrium Theory
- Festinger's Cognitive Dissonance Theory
- Behavioral Learning Theory

There are several theories that are called need theories. What they have in common is that they state that human beings are motivated by needs. If needs are unmet, the person would be most motivated to do something that would meet that need.

Maslow's Need Theory

Abraham Maslow (1971) believed that human beings are basically good and that they innately move toward higher levels of functioning as their lower-level needs are met. One reason this view of human nature is so important is that if humans were not basically good, one would not expect them to improve on their own. Later theories that will be discussed will take a different view of human nature and, logically, will support different motivational strategies. In a nutshell, Maslow described needs at five levels, going from the most basic physiological needs to the highest, most selfless needs (see figure 5.1). He believed that every person has the same hierarchy of needs, which is usually presented in a triangular graphic going from a broad base of basic needs to an apex of lofty, rarely met needs. Each set of needs from the base to the top must be met in order (i.e., the physiological needs must be met to experience safety needs, and both must be met before love and belonging needs are felt). These needs are shown in figure 5.1, and examples of each follow here:

Physiological Needs: to have air, water, food, sleep, elimination, sex

Safety Needs: to escape fear and pain, to have physical security, order, physical safety

Belonging and Love Needs: to love and be loved, to have friends, to be part of a family

Self-esteem Needs: to feel competent, independent, successful, respected, and worthwhile

Self-actualization Needs: to be one's true self, to achieve one's highest potential, to want knowledge and wisdom, to be able to understand and accept oneself and others, to be creative and appreciative of beauty in the world

What are the implications of this theory for homeschooling? First, the theory indicates that it is necessary to adequately satisfy one's basic needs before one can turn to meeting needs higher in the hierarchy. For example, if a child is hungry, it is very hard for him or her to memorize spelling words. But once a person has taken care of the needs at levels 1 and 2, then one is free, and in fact motivated, to search for love, then self-esteem, and then finally self-actualization. Therefore, in Maslow's opinion, if someone is struggling to achieve a goal, the possibility should be considered that some more basic need still remains unmet and must be satisfied first. While Maslow's theory makes intuitive sense, research has not supported the theory that all needs at a more primary level must be satisfied before moving on to higher needs. However, it would not hurt to try to analyze whether there may be some unmet needs if a child is struggling with motivation for schoolwork.

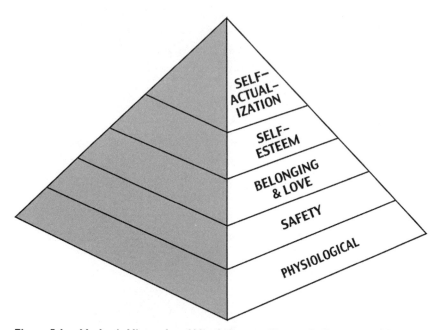

Figure 5.1. Maslow's Hierarchy of Needs (source: Tanner P. Clements, 2003)

Murray's Needs Theory

According to Murray (1938, 1943), a person with an unmet need will be tense or uncomfortable until the need is met, then would feel less tense after it is met. He saw motivation as the desire either to avoid or to release tension. Unlike Maslow, he believed those things that cause tension vary from person to person. Therefore, things that motivate people would differ from person to person. Murray listed twenty different needs that we can have, but as is clear in the earlier chapter on personality, asking ten different theorists would result in ten different lists. Murray believed that people are motivated by different needs and to different degrees. His are listed here, in the following paragraphs, more for interest and for broadening what most people think of as the range of possible motivators than as a definitive list. Some of them actually sound somewhat strange, but that does not mean they are not true.

Abasement: the need to surrender. Example: A dog immediately rolls over and shows its belly when a bigger dog comes around. A husband says "yes, dear" when his wife disagrees with him, even though he doesn't really agree with her. A potential application: A student may give up easily when work becomes difficult.

Achievement: the need to overcome obstacles. Example: A student is told that no one ever makes an A in "Dr. Meanie's" class, so the student takes the class, studies for hours, and earns an A, just to prove that it can be done. A potential application: These types make great students wherever they are. However, they may have to be encouraged to relax occasionally.

Affiliation: the need to form friendships and associations. Example: A student joins several clubs because she just loves to be around people and do things with friends. A potential application: These students will miss school friends. Other social outlets should be found and can be used as motivators: "Finish your work and you can have a friend over."

Aggression: the need to assault or injure. Example: A bully. Need I say more? A potential application: Other parents will be thrilled this child is being homeschooled. However, the parent may become the victim.

Autonomy: the need to resist influence or coercion. Example: Someone about to have a medical procedure wants to know all the facts and make the decisions about it without being "sold" by the physician. A potential application: This child may need to be convinced of the benefit of the work he or she is being asked to do. At the extreme, this person may be stubborn.

Counteraction: the need to proudly refuse admission of defeat. Example: A tennis player who uses the excuse of tennis elbow, poor-fitting shoes, or bad calls as the reason for the loss of a tennis match. A potential application: Sometimes helping a child practice losing gracefully is beneficial. Once the child is old enough, the necessity of admitting defeat can be taught.

Deference: the need to admire and willingly follow. Example: A sheep. Also, political campaign workers or rock band groupies could fall in this category. These are the followers in the world. A potential application: If the child feels this way about the homeschooling parent, this could make a wonderful teacher–student relationship. If not, sometimes the accomplishments of an admired person could be held out as a goal for the student.

Defendance: the need to defend oneself against blame or belittlement. Example: "It wasn't my fault. Here is why it appears that it was, but that was obviously a difference in perspective." A potential application: If it doesn't matter, sometimes it's easier to go on than to force a confession out of a child like this. This doesn't mean not to address the wrong with consequences, because the child probably does know he or she is wrong. The words are just difficult to say. However, if this is an ongoing trend of not taking responsibility, it may need to be addressed. This will be covered in the chapter on discipline.

Dominance: the need to influence or control others. Example: Most politicians and many bosses fall in this category. They are the ones who boss the deference folks around. A potential application: A child who is high in this need could be a difficult child to homeschool. The parents have to stay on their toes to retain control.

Exhibition: the need to attract attention to one's person. Example: The guy at the party who dances on the table with the lampshade on his head. The class clown would also qualify. A potential application: Just giving them attention can motivate these children. In a classroom, the child might be distracting, but in homeschooling, the parent's attention may be useful for keeping the child motivated. If the parent isn't naturally encouraging, however, it should be developed.

Harmavoidance: the need to avoid pain or physical injury. Example: We "chickens" fall in this category. Some people are warier than others. A potential application: If the child perceives something as risky, he is unlikely to be motivated to try it. Most homeschooling activities aren't physically painful, but many children who avoid physical pain may avoid risks in other areas as well. Some difficult academic tasks could be perceived as risky.

Infavoidance: the need to avoid failure, shame, or humiliation. Example: A student who has to be right. They may have to practice a speech five hours a day, but they will to avoid the embarrassment of messing up. A potential application: Unless it's taken to the extreme, this characteristic is very beneficial for schoolwork. However, the child can become too fearful and avoid trying some activities just because of the fear of failure.

Nurturance: the need to nourish, aid, or protect. Example: A mommy. These are the people who go around taking care of the succorance folks listed later. A potential application: These children are helpful to have at home. Don't abuse their help because it interferes with school time.

Order: the need to arrange and organize. Example: At the extreme this could be an obsessive-compulsive person who files spices alphabetically. A potential application: These children are generally pleasant to homeschool because schoolwork stays neat, they can find their assignments, and they typically follow instructions.

Play: the need to relax and amuse oneself. Example: These are the people who really enjoy golfing, amusement parks, and napping. A potential application: Most children have this tendency. If this need is too strong, some strong motivational strategies should be used to get them to do schoolwork.

Rejection: the need to snub, ignore, or exclude. Example: These people make themselves feel better by belittling someone else. A potential application: In a school setting, this child would be a snob. In homeschooling, there is little chance for this with peers. However, if the child has limited social activities, he or she may need to be discouraged from such activity, or he or she will have few friends.

Sentience: the need to seek and enjoy sensuous pleasure. This is sensuous meaning *sensation* (touching, seeing, hearing). These people like to listen to good music, watch good music, or get a massage. A potential application: These children may benefit from hands-on activities and perhaps listening to music while studying.

Sex: the need to form and further an erotic relationship. They just like sex; no example is necessary. Hopefully sex will not be needed as a motivator during homeschooling.

Succorance: the need to seek aid, protection, or sympathy. Example: This is the person who likes to be protected by a big, strong person. These are the people who will be taken care of by the nurturance folks listed earlier. A potential application: These children typically like being homeschooled as long as they have a nurturing parent doing the homeschooling. However, they may overreact to illness or rejection.

Understanding: the need to analyze experience. Example: This is a knowledge junkie (I know because I am one). It's not enough to know *that* something happened. These folks want to know *why* it happened, *how* it can be made to happen differently next time, and *who* is responsible. A potential application: Children who are high in this need are easy to teach in any setting.

It is helpful to keep two things in mind when reading through this list. First, this is a theory, so these are not all necessarily needs nor is the list necessarily exhaustive. Second, the parent must look at his or her own motivators, as well as the child's.

Achievement Motivation Theory

Achievement motivation (Atkinson and Feather, 1966; McClelland, 1961) is the likelihood that someone actually will perform a task. The theory has to do with someone's need or tendency to approach goals and the need or tendency to avoid failure, coupled with the payoff for success and the potential negative consequences of failure. Atkinson even developed a mathematical formula to demonstrate how these tendencies are related. If these tendencies could be measured, the amount of achievement motivation for a task could be predicted with the following formula (those who like math will love this, and those who hate math will be relieved because the formula has no numbers):

Tendency to approach a goal = probability of success × incentive value of success × innate need for achievement

Tendency to avoid failure = probability of failure × incentive value of
failure × innate need for achievement

Resultant achievement motivation = tendency to approach a goal −
tendency to avoid failure

In the formula, the incentive value of success means what the reward for
succeeding is likely to be. Incentive value of failure is what the negative
result for failing is likely to be. If the resultant achievement motivation is
a positive number, then the person is motivated to do whatever the task
is. If it is a negative number (if the avoidance of failure outweighs the tendency to approach the task), the person is not motivated to do the task.

Research on achievement motivation has shown that people who have
high achievement motivation become less motivated when they experience success but more motivated when they experience failure. For a
person with low achievement motivation, it is just the opposite (see
table 5.1).

What are some applications of this theory? Reducing someone's fear
of or avoidance of failure rather than trying to increase the value of the
desired activity can sometimes increase motivation, as can showing
someone that there is a probability of success. If there is not a very good
probability of success for an activity, teaching, training, or otherwise giving the person tools that will increase the probability of success should
be motivating. Giving someone who is naturally an unmotivated person
a taste of success or giving someone who is naturally a motivated person
a taste of failure may increase motivation. Finally, in order to increase
the incentive value of success, the payoff can be increased. This will be
discussed more thoroughly in the section on behavioral theories of motivation later in the chapter.

The following theories are referred to as non-need theories.

Table 5.1.   Applications of Atkinson's Achievement Motivation Theory

	Achievement	Motivation
	High Achievement Motivation	Low Achievement Motivation
Success	motivation decreases	motivation increases
	(no challenge)	(a taste of success)
Failure	motivation increases	motivation decreases
	(challenge)	(learned helplessness)

Attribution Theory

Attribution theory involves assessing how people perceive the causes of their success or failure in achievement situations. Some people will attribute success to luck, some to ability, some to task difficulty, and some to effort. All of us tend to attribute our successes to internal causes (we take the credit) and our failures to external causes (we blame others or circumstances). Beyond that, people differ in the attributions they make. The main categories used in discussions of academics are shown in table 5.2 and described here:

Ability. This is internal because it is within the person. For example, IQ and prior learning, as discussed in an earlier chapter, are stable because a person currently has as much as he or she currently has.

Effort. This is internal because it is the person in question who either puts forth the effort or not. It is unstable because someone may try harder on some occasions than others.

Task Difficulty. This has to do with the inherent difficulty of the task at hand. It is external because someone else determines the difficulty of most tasks with which a person is faced. For example, the teacher makes the test as hard as it is. Task difficulty is stable because an individual task is as hard as it is. It doesn't vary.

Luck. This has to do with some force in the universe that either enhances or inhibits performance. It is external because the person has no control over it and unstable because (if such a thing actually exists) it varies from person to person and task to task.

The most favored of these attributions for schoolchildren or anyone to believe is effort. That is the only one over which we have control. The other three are either not changeable (stable) or outside our control (external) or both. Therefore, the most beneficial thing for homeschooled children is to demonstrate the relationship between effort and success. Sometimes they have to be challenged to try hard enough to result in an improvement in success, however.

Table 5.2. Attributions of Success and Failure

	Stable	Unstable
Internal locus of control	ability	effort
External locus of control	task difficulty	luck

Piaget's Disequilibrium Theory

Jean Piaget's theory of how children learn (Piaget and Inhelder, 1969) was already discussed in chapter 1, but one part of that theory is particularly pertinent to the discussion of motivation. Piaget believed that children are naturally motivated to learn and adapt when faced with something they don't understand. He called this state of not understanding *disequilibrium*. The term came from equilibrium, which is used often in biology and chemistry to mean that something is stable or in balance. Piaget said that children were in balance or in a state of equilibrium when they understand or are not confused. However, when confused or unsure they experience disequilibrium and are uncomfortable until they do understand and return to that state of equilibrium.

The application of this theory would be to have children faced with questions, problems, or material that makes them curious. Piaget would cringe at the thought of teachers or homeschooling parents handing a child a list of words or facts to memorize. Instead, he would encourage children to discover concepts and seek out answers to problems.

Festinger's Cognitive Dissonance Theory

Without elaborating very much on this theory (Festinger, 1957), the gist of it is that people have difficulty behaving inconsistently with their beliefs about themselves. If someone thinks of him- or herself as an honest person and finds that something he or she said was incorrect, the person will typically be uncomfortable until what was said is corrected. An alternative way of handling this inconsistency would be for the person to change his or her self-image as an honest person, but that would be more uncomfortable. The primary application of this theory is that a homeschooling parent should create expectations in the child for the kind of behavior that is desired. If a child can be convinced that she is a high achiever, she may begin to act like one.

A risk is that children know when we are and are not being truthful. If a child has failed frequently in math and the parent says, "You are a great mathematician," all that will be accomplished is that the child will no longer believe the parent. However, if the comment is more accurate, the child may begin to believe.

Behavioral Learning Theory

The same principles covered earlier in this book on behavioral learning theory apply here. Skinner (1953) and other behaviorists teach that through appropriate reinforcement, punishment, and extinction, people will do what someone wants them to do. This often takes diagnosing what is reinforcing to them and what is punishing to them, but, if done correctly, it is extremely effective and has decades of research support to back up that claim. Of all the theories covered, behaviorism has been shown to be most effective. How does one do this?

- Children should be reinforced for doing what the parents want them to do. Grown-ups get paid to work. Shouldn't there be a payoff for schoolwork? This does not have to be monetary, but if there is absolutely no good reason the child can see for doing the work, he or she won't be motivated to do it.
- Appropriate behaviors should be modeled. For example, watching television while telling a child to go read a book will probably not be terribly motivating. If a child sees the parent reading for pleasure, he will be more likely to read for pleasure.
- If a behavior is already intrinsically motivated, it shouldn't be extrinsically motivated. An intrinsically motivated behavior is one that is already being done just because the child likes to do it. Occasional verbal praise would be fine, but research has shown that adding some kind of extrinsic reward (money, ice cream) for an activity the person is already motivated to do will actually reduce their intrinsic motivation.
- If the child is not motivated he or she should be given some type of extrinsic motivation. There can be either some consequence for not doing schoolwork (repeating a test until it is passed at an acceptable level) or some reward for completing schoolwork (having some free time if they study and do well the first time).

APPLICATIONS OF MOTIVATION THEORIES

It is not so important that a homeschooling parent remember which theorist is responsible for which aspect of motivation theory. It is important to have a variety of motivational tools in the bag of tricks. Listed below are practical, usable applications of the motivation theories described in this chapter and ideas from other research on motivation that are not specifically tied to a particular theory. They are listed in no certain order.

- Modeling task-related thinking and problem solving
- Showing enthusiasm; enthusiastic teachers are very motivating
- Providing warmth and empathy
- Setting high expectations
- Inducing dissonance
- Inducing curiosity
- Setting clear goals
- Providing feedback
- Helping students think about how they think and learn and figuring out what motivates them
- Personalizing content; use examples pertinent to the student
- Using challenging material; too easy gets boring
- Providing reinforcement
- Emphasizing cause-and-effect relationship between effort and success
- Addressing fear of failure
- Varying format
- Providing order and safety
- Communicating expectations

Some of these may seem completely unrelated to theories given previously in this chapter; however, all have sound research support. There are likely dozens more bullets that could be included, but for the sake of brevity, these will suffice.

DISCIPLINE

A challenge to classroom teachers as well as homeschooling parents is maintaining an effective learning environment. The topic is so vast that entire books and college courses are devoted to it. For that reason, the highlights and practical applications will be given without exhaustive coverage. The material in this chapter is broadly applicable to many areas of parenting, not just homeschooling.

Discipline can mean many things. It includes developing and enforcing rules, problem solving, and refers to what the parent does and what the child develops. Below are some descriptions of the most common theories. These apply to maintaining order in traditional classrooms as well as homeschool "classrooms."

BEHAVIORAL TECHNIQUES

Earlier in this book, behaviorism was described in relation to learning and motivation, and the strong research support for its effectiveness was emphasized. The very same principles can be applied to maintaining appropriate behavior. There are some principles drawn from behavioral learning theory that apply quite nicely to any type of learning or teaching situation.

Convey Expectations

Expectations can be spoken, written and posted, or written as a contract for the involved parties to sign. Rules and consequences for breaking those rules should be specified.

Reinforce Compliance

When the rules are followed, a simple "good job" or "thanks for doing that" goes a long way toward having them followed in the future. If good behavior is not recognized, children may behave badly just to get the attention. Other more obvious reinforcers are useful as well. Here is a list of possible activity reinforcers:

- Go with your child and participate in his or her favorite activity
- Take the child to lunch
- Sit and talk with the child uninterrupted
- Go to the park, play a game, go to the zoo or another fun place

A list of tangible reinforcers:

- Small toy
- Stickers
- Larger toy after completing a specific number of the behaviors
- A homemade certificate identifying the accomplishment

A list of edible reinforcers:

- Candy
- A favorite meal for dinner
- A favorite dessert
- Cheese goldfish crackers
- Ice cream

And a list of social reinforcers:

- Someone saying "good job!"
- A hug
- A pat on the back
- A thumbs-up

Punish Noncompliance

Noncompliance should be followed with some type of negative consequence. If it is not, there is no motivation to comply. Most children do not just wake up one day and say, "Hey, I really need to apply myself to my schoolwork. I think I'll stop goofing off and work hard today." It would be a nice surprise, though. There has to be some looming consequence if the students don't do their work.

If behavioral principles are followed consistently, and the reinforcers and punishers are strong enough, children will be compliant. Consistency is the most difficult but most effective part of the equation.

KOUNIN'S CLASSROOM MANAGEMENT

The main premise behind Kounin's (1970) ideas about classroom management is that teaching situations should be set up to prevent misbehavior from happening. His philosophy is that if the teacher keeps the children engaged in their work and knows everything that is going on at all times, there will be few, if any behavior problems. This has typically been applied to classroom teachers, but works well for homeschoolers. Kounin coined several terms to guide teachers.

Organization

The teacher should have things so organized that everyone, including the children, knows what is expected. No time should be lost looking for things or giving instructions about what to do next. A certain routine for each day of the week is very helpful, even if Mondays are different from Tuesdays, which are different from Wednesdays. That keeps the kids from asking questions such as "do we have to do math today?" They will know if that is a day they do math.

Overlapping

This is the ability to do two or more things at the same time. In a classroom, it could be evidenced by the teacher overseeing seatwork while running a reading group. With a homeschooling parent, it could be evidenced by working one on one with one child while doing laundry or making sure a second child is completing the test he or she is supposed to be taking.

Withitness

Isn't this a hip 1960s word? What Kounin meant by this is that the teachers (or parents) have to have "eyes in the backs of their heads." They need to be able to know what is going on with all of the children at all times. Even if the parent doesn't really know, he or she has to be able to make the child think he or she does. Many times my husband has shared something with our children that they had no idea how he knew, and he would just remind them, "You know, Mom and I know everything." They used to believe it. I'm not sure if they still do.

Preventing Problems

While preventing problems is the main idea of Kounin's theory, it also deserves a category of its own. Trying to think of all the things that could go wrong is how problems are prevented. If children are in a room out of sight, could they hurt one another, cheat, or distract one another from working? If so, they can be moved so they can be seen. Is one of the desk chairs so comfortable that the child may doze off? A less comfortable chair can be used. Is the pencil sharpener somewhere where the child loses a lot of work time or gets distracted going to sharpen a pencil? It can be moved or lots of sharp pencils can be provided.

Momentum

Faster seems to be better in whatever learning situation people are engaged. If lessons move too slowly, there is the opportunity to daydream, get in trouble, or forget. A nice steady pace seems to keep students' attention and keep them out of trouble. However, moving too quickly could prevent them from learning the concept at all. In homeschooling, there is the freedom to speed up and slow down. That freedom can be used to the child's advantage. If the student finishes work and does not have anything else assigned, yet the parent wants him or her to continue working, extra activites should be available and known to the student. Here are some suggestions that he or she could do to fill his or her extra time.

- Check completed work for errors
- Work ahead so that less work can be done the next day/week
- Read a book or magazine
- Write a poem, story, or journal entry
- Help a struggling sibling
- Tidy up
- Study for a test
- Practice something that is an area of weakness (math problems, spelling words)
- Write notes to a friend or out-of-town relative

This list or one similar can be provided for the student so he or she cannot say, "There was nothing else for me to do."

Smooth Transitions

Transitions from one subject to another should be practiced. If children always do language arts after math, they can be taught the routine of putting away the math book, math notebook, calculator, and pencils, and taking out the language book, language notebook, and a pen. That way they do not have to scramble around thinking, "Gee, I wonder what I'll do next and what I'll need?"

INTERVENTION

If it becomes necessary to intervene and change a child's behavior, some principles should be kept in mind.

Brevity

Briefer is better. For example, if looking at a child with the *evil eye* will stop his or her behavior, studying will be interrupted much less than if a loud lecture about why the behavior was wrong is given.

Consistency

Punishment should consistently follow broken rules, praise should consistently follow obeyed rules, and rules should stay the same. If children know what to expect, they will be less likely to misbehave.

Continuum of Intervention

The least obtrusive or interfering intervention that is effective should be used when a child is not following the rules. However, if some sort of mild punishment is used that doesn't work and it is followed by gradually more severe interventions, ultimately a harsher intervention may have to be used than would originally have been effective.

For example, there is a familiar adage that says if you throw a frog into a pot of boiling water he will hop out, but if you put him in cool water and gradually turn it up, he will stay in and cook. This is the same principle with gradually increasing punishments. Sometimes it is best to have one that is harsh enough to get the child's attention the first time.

Following is a list of some interventions that work well in the classroom, in the homeschool classroom, in Sunday school, at a department store, and a host of other places, organized from the least obtrusive to the most obtrusive:

Ignore. Ignoring a behavior that is not dangerous is effective if the purpose of the behavior is to seek attention. Tantrums, pouting, and whining generally fall into this category.

Praise. Praising the behavior of someone who is exhibiting appropriate behavior may motivate the misbehaver to change. For example, to get Sue-Sue, who keeps getting out of her seat, to stay seated, comment on another child's behavior by saying something like, "I like the way you are sitting quietly in your seat, Vic-Vic."

Give "Death Stare" or "Evil Eye." Mothers are particularly good at this. It is a disapproving facial expression that tells the child that he or she had better stop whatever he or she is doing or suffer the consequences. It will only work if he or she knows that the person "staring" will follow through with consequences.

Point or Gesture. This works very similarly to the "stare" above. It could consist of just pointing to the child or wagging one finger toward them (the international sign for "no-no"). Some parents and teachers use a finger snap. The purpose is to get the children's attention, let them know they have been seen, let them know their behavior is inappropriate, and if they continue there will be consequences.

Touch. Touching the child (usually lightly on the shoulder) will remind them to get back to work.

Re-involve (Ask a Question). This is used more in a classroom setting but can be applied to homeschooling if the parent is actually teaching aloud. For example, two children are passing notes in the back of the class. The teacher calls one of their names and asks a question about the current topic. Usually, the child will not know the answer and the embarrassment serves to punish the behavior. Just being pointed out tends to bring their attention back to the class.

Directly Tell the Person to Stop the Behavior. For example, "Johnny, stop pulling Matilda's hair right now."

Threaten a Consequence If the Behavior Does Not Stop. For example, "If you do not finish your math by 11:00 a.m., you can't go to the mall today."

Follow Through with the Threatened Consequence Immediately If the Behavior Does Not Stop. If the child does not finish his or her math by 11:00 a.m., he or she does not go to the mall.

WHAT NOT TO DO

It is just as important to know what not to do when disciplining children. Here is a list of things that are either not very effective or are not ethical to use as discipline interventions:

- Repeating commands over and over
- Yelling
- Saying "I'm the boss and you're not!"
- Having to have the last word
- Clenching fists or teeth
- Embarrassing or ridiculing the child
- Being sarcastic
- Criticizing the person instead of the behavior

- Using physical force unless there is absolutely no alternative
- Drawing unrelated persons into the conflict
- Begging
- Saying, "You always . . ." or, "You never . . ."
- Comparing the child to some *better* child
- Holding a grudge
- Nagging
- Losing your cool
- Mimicking the student
- Changing the rules

At the risk of being overly simplistic, the best philosophy of discipline is to establish rules, teach the rules, punish broken rules, and praise the child when the rules are kept.

TESTING AND GRADING

Testing and grading actually serve two purposes. The first is to give the parent an idea of how well the child is learning the material being covered. The second is to motivate the child to put forth effort as he or she does schoolwork. This is true for homeschooling as well as traditional schooling. How many students would apply themselves if there were no evaluation? My college students assure me that very few would.

The first assumption made in this chapter is that homeschooling parents want to verify and document their children's learning. If not, this chapter can be skipped. This is not said tongue in cheek, because there are families who practice un-schooling who don't wish to grade or formally evaluate academic learning because they do not differentiate academic learning from day-to-day learning. This chapter covers the pros and cons of various ways to assess and document learning. Some of the aspects discussed include ease of use and effectiveness of various types of evaluation. Characteristics of good evaluation instruments are discussed, as are cautions about the use of various types of testing and evaluation methods. Evaluation of learning seems like a rather straightforward process on the surface. However, making sure that the type of learning that is to be measured is actually being measured accurately is quite a complex process. This is not the place for a chapter on the academic study of measurement, but some of the issues inherent in verifying learning need to be addressed. I will try to keep it simple.

TO TEST OR NOT TO TEST

The first choice is whether or not to test. There are some homeschooling families as well as teachers in public and private schools and colleges who prefer not to test. There are other ways to assess learning. This can be done through informal oral questioning, assigning activities that have students use the skills they have been studying (e.g., have a geometry student build something that requires the use of angular measurements), or writing papers about what has been learned.

However, if a parent is not opposed to testing, it can be used to efficiently learn how well material is being covered, how effective teaching materials are, and how much effort the kids are putting forth. Therefore, if a parent chooses to test, there are choices as to how to go about that.

Buying Tests with the Curriculum

Buying ready-made tests is by far the easiest way to go. Some curriculum materials have better tests than others. Some come with the tests completely written, ready to go, with an answer key. Others have test books from which the teacher or parent picks items to use and constructs tests from the items provided. These vary in quality. It is best to talk to various people about what they did and did not like about the various curriculum materials they have used.

Writing Tests

It is much more difficult to write tests, but doing so gives more control over the content covered and the quality. One thing that makes test writing so difficult is that it takes a high level of familiarity with the content, which may not seem so difficult in the younger grades but becomes quite difficult in the upper grades. The parent may have known it or could relearn it easily, but he or she is not up on it enough to write tests. In order to write a good test, the parent has to know the material better than the student does. At those younger ages when the parent is doing a great deal of direct instruction anyway, that familiarity is there, and writing some or all tests may be preferable. In fact, if one is working with a child daily, informal oral testing may be preferred to giving a formal paper–pencil test.

If the decision is made to write tests, some or all, there are some considerations that should be followed.

Content. A little of most topics that have been covered should be included. Every little thing does not need to be tested, especially with older children. If there are certain skill areas that have been covered, it is best to have an item or more in each of those skill areas. For example, if long division and two-digit multiplication have been covered in math, the test should contain at least some of each of these types of problems.

Length. A test should not be unreasonably long or the student will get frustrated and tired, and the teacher will wear out writing it and grading it. However, if it is too brief, important concepts may be missed.

Age Appropriateness. The age of the child should be considered when preparing tests. Size of print, length of sentences, difficulty of language, and the type of thinking required all should be considered. Print should be larger and sentences simpler for young children. Remember from the chapter on learning that Piaget believed children could not understand abstract concepts until at least age eleven, if not later. If that is true, it would not be fair to include abstract material in a test for younger children.

Clarity. Clarity is always a struggle. A question that seems perfectly clear at the time it is written may seem very ambiguous to the student. It is generally a good idea to have students explain why they chose answers that they did on tests to determine if their response was actually legitimate. Numerous times this has happened in my college teaching. I intend a question to be read one way, but a student will point out that it could be interpreted a different but correct way.

Objectivity. The more objective questions are (meaning they have a right or wrong answer with no gray area), the more easily they can be graded. It is difficult for parents to take points off on a subjective item. The temptation is to give the benefit of the doubt. Objective items alleviate this temptation. This does not mean that the use of essay questions and open-ended questions should be eliminated, but that their use should be limited. Additionally, even the grading of subjective items can be made more objective. Before grading, the parent can determine what the characteristics of a well-answered question would be. This is called a scoring rubric. For example, if a child is asked to describe two positive and two negative implications of taxation, then the parent would look for those four implications in the answer. If only three were given, points would be deducted.

Expectations. Students should know before and during a test what is expected of them. If chapter 10 should be studied, that should be said. If they should write one paragraph, one paragraph should be asked for. If they are to circle *all that apply,* they should be told that. Testing is not a cruel game of "see whether we can trick the student." Testing should confirm that students have learned the information they were expected to learn. If they have been warned what that will be, they are likely to be motivated to study that material.

GRADING

As mentioned earlier in this chapter, some homeschooling parents may choose to forgo the use of grades. However, most will want to keep up with grades in some form or fashion to look at progress over the long term. Some school systems do not require the reporting of grades at the elementary level but do require it at the high school level. If a homeschooler is registered with some type of umbrella organization, that organization may require grade reporting. Also, for college admission, a grade point average (GPA) generally must be reported. There are several methods for calculating or reporting grades.

Grading Scales

Letter Grades. By far, most people use this type of grading. The most typical is 90–100 percent for an A, 80–89 percent for a B, and so on. However, it is up to the parent's discretion whether to use this scale or alter it somewhat. Some curriculum materials use much higher cutoff scores (94 for an A, 86 for a B, and so on). Not only can the cutoff scores differ greatly, how these grades are determined can also vary. Some may administer a few objective tests and average the scores. Others may assign papers, orally examine the child, and have children do hands-on projects. Some parents may have students rework tests or assignments to improve their grades, while others do not.

Primary importance should be placed on whether or not the child has learned the material assigned. However, in the real world, scholarships and honors come attached to GPA. The homeschooling parents have to choose how to address this for themselves.

Pass/Fail. Giving pass/fail grades (or satisfactory/unsatisfactory) rather than letter grades is simpler than assigning letter grades. A cutoff would be set to be considered passing. If the student met or surpassed the cutoff he or she would pass. The main problem with pass/fail grading is that a GPA cannot be determined from it, and therefore it cannot be used for determining eligibility for scholarships.

No Grades. This is probably not an option by high school level, but at the earlier grades it is, unless a state or umbrella organization has specific rules that require the assignment of grades. I, personally, feel the teacher and the student need the feedback that grades provide.

Material on Which Grades Are Based

Tests Only. Grades can be determined using whatever types of evaluation strategies the teacher chooses to use. Some prefer using only test scores. Seatwork, daily assignments, and homework would not count in this grade. The benefit to this is that there may be less grading for the teacher, and students are given time (in the way of other assignments) to prepare for the tests; however, students may not try as hard on assignments they know will not be graded.

All Assignments. Every assignment, or at least most assignments, can be included in a grade. This would include tests, seatwork, homework, workbooks, and whatever else. The benefit of using many sources of information is that students know work will be graded and will work harder, and one or two terrible test scores will not jeopardize their grade. The drawback is that there is much more grading to do.

Timing of Grades

Many school systems use six-week grading cycles. Some use nine weeks, and others report only semester grades. The choice of the timing of grades will be largely determined by the curriculum used and any umbrella organization under which the homeschooler is registered. Some curriculum materials are broken into six weeks; some, nine; and some, semesters. Yet others have no natural breakdown, and the teacher has to determine this.

Most students, whether homeschooled or traditionally schooled, receive semester grades, even if they don't use six-week or nine-week grades. For high school, it is the semester grade for each course that is typically reported.

Calculating Grades

I know from teaching college statistics and supervising teachers that tasks like calculating the percentage correct on an assignment or an average grade may petrify some parents and teachers. For that reason, following are instructions on calculating percentages and weighting items:

Calculating Percentage Correct. To determine the percentage of items correct on anything, divide the number correct by the number possible and multiply by 100. For example, for a 25-item test, if the student correctly answered 20 items: $20 \div 25 = .80$ and $.80 \times 100 = 80\%$.

Weighting Items. To weight an item to be included in a grade such as a semester grade, multiply the grade received by the weighting percentage.

As an example, if a final exam should count as 25% of the final grade and the student received 85% on the final exam, $85 \times .25 = 21.25$. If a term paper should count as 50% of the final grade and the student received 90% on the term paper, then 90 × .50 = 45. If homework should count as 25% of the final grade and a student received 100% for homework, then 100 × .25 = 25.

To calculate the final grade for the three examples above, add the weighted grades: 21.25 + 45 + 25 = 91.25. The semester grade would be 91.25%.

8

PHYSICAL ENVIRONMENT

Such simple topics as what types of furniture to provide for home-schooling, organization of materials, and whether children should be separated for school are covered in this chapter. The attempt is to cover the research on learning environments in understandable terms and to incorporate previous experience.

The learning area should be set up to reduce distractions, increase convenience, and enhance "withitness." The area should be convenient for the students as well as the teacher. The primary considerations include designing work space, storing materials, and keeping distractions to a minimum.

WORK SPACE

The work spaces should fit the children. Some questions to be asked include: Can they write comfortably? Is there room for a book and notebook? Are the chairs so uncomfortable that they cannot sit still? Are the chairs so comfortable that they fall asleep? Is there enough light to see well?

If the homeschooling work space will be used for other activities, there is a risk that schoolwork will be lost or damaged. A plan can be made for how to put away schoolwork to lessen this likelihood.

MATERIALS STORAGE AND ACCESSIBILITY

There should be ample storage space that is close enough so as not to distract other children or to interrupt the child's work in order to get needed books or supplies. The materials should also be organized enough that the student can find what is needed, when it is needed. This does not mean that the parent should be solely responsible for this organization. As a part of school, the student can be taught organization, neatness, and responsibility for materials.

NOISE

Noise may or may not be distracting to a child. In public school there is often a great deal of noise, and school goes on. Therefore, a silent environment is neither required nor expected for homeschooling. However, some students may be distracted by noises, particularly other siblings and televisions. Some accommodation may have to be made to reduce the noise or to move the student farther from the source of the noise if it hinders schoolwork.

A second aspect related to the topic of noise concerns how much noise students will be allowed to make. Just as public and private school teachers differ in the amount of noise they will allow, homeschooling parents and children differ in their willingness to tolerate noise. Some parents and students may be comfortable with a great deal of talking and interaction. Others may require near silence. This should be addressed as rules are made, but the characteristics of the parties involved should be considered as these rules are made.

SIGHTS

Is there a window with a beautiful view of a playground right outside the work area? Many sights can be distracting to homeschooled students, just as they can to traditionally schooled students. Considering what sights might be distracting and placing the work area away from that view should reduce the temptation to daydream.

SUPERVISION

If children are out of the way of household distractions, they may also be out of the way of adult supervision. There needs to be a way to ensure that students stay on task, do not cheat, and do not interfere with one another as they do their schoolwork. Sometimes it is worth having them weather a few distractions in order to keep a closer eye on them.

We began our adventure into homeschooling by setting up a room dedicated to school. Each child had a desk, chair, pencils, pens, bookshelf, and storage cabinet, and they shared a wastebasket. There was a large marker board on the wall that was filled in with their assignments for the day, and a clock hung by it so they would know when to change subjects. It was in a finished basement, so it had a comfortable temperature, no windows with beautiful scenery beckoning, and it was far from the television, washing machine, and telephone. How ideal we thought that would be. The beauty of this arrangement would be that the teacher could periodically check on progress, but the remainder of the time would be spent in silent self-study . . . or not. Our children daydreamed, bickered, and even on occasion cheated during this arrangement.

We decided that more supervision, even with its potential distractions, was preferable. School was conducted at the dining room table after that, with one child at one end of the table and the other child at the other end. There are distractions: the television, two little brothers, the dishwasher, and the telephone. However, there is also a father who walks by and says, "You're daydreaming. Get back to work." This has been a far more successful arrangement for our children and for us. It is apparent that a great deal of homeschooling, even down to the physical arrangement, is specific to the personalities in the family that is homeschooling.

SCHEDULING

Whether or not to follow a schedule and, if so, what type of schedule to follow are addressed in this chapter. If a family practices un-schooling, as described in the chapter on curriculum, then they will most likely have no formal schedule. Other homeschooling parents may also choose to have no schedule, while the remainder will range from flexible to quite rigid in their scheduling. Two types of scheduling are discussed in this chapter, as are the benefits and drawbacks of each.

TRADITIONAL FORMAL SCHEDULING

Homeschooling can be organized as a traditional public or private school day. Students can begin school at a specified time (e.g., 8:00 a.m.), break for lunch at noon, and complete school at 3:00 p.m., devoting approximately fifty-five minutes to each subject. While this is predictable and would allow plenty of time for coverage of material, it also is several hours more than the school attendance requirement of homeschoolers in most states. It also would infringe on the flexibility that is so appealing with homeschooling.

FLEXIBLE SCHEDULING

An alternative to traditional formal scheduling is flexible scheduling. This could take many forms. One possibility would be to have the students complete one lesson or some other preset amount of material in each subject each day. If lessons were completed quickly, the school day would end early. If not, the school day would end late. This arrangement gives the students a degree of control over how long their school days are. We have used this type of flexible scheduling with our children who have worked on schoolwork until 6:00 in the evening some days because they played around during school time. The danger in this arrangement is that students may hurry through material without taking the time to gain a thorough understanding of it. However, this can be offset by holding the students accountable using some kind of assessment to verify that they have learned the material (see the chapter on testing and grading).

Other types of flexible scheduling include covering some subjects on some days of the week and other subjects on other days of the week, or requiring students to complete a certain amount of work in a certain time frame. For example, students may have an assignment due at the end of the week, but it is up to the students to decide when they will do the work.

Characteristics of the people involved should be considered when deciding how scheduled to be. If one of the children functions best with predictability, then a schedule will be welcomed. If the parent or children have other obligations, more scheduling will be required so they can meet those other obligations.

We have found it most helpful to designate 8:30 a.m. to 1:00 p.m. as school time so that we can protect it by not arranging other activities during this time. If something comes up, then the time lost can be made up at another time. (For example, our daughter babysat for a ladies' Bible study on Tuesday mornings. On those days she babysat in the morning, came home, ate lunch, and did schoolwork from noon to 4:00 p.m.)

SUMMARY

I hope this book has not only produced questions in the mind of the reader but has answered many as well. The number of decisions to be made before leaping into homeschooling seems daunting. However, there are many resources available that can help in that decision-making process. There are many books on the market that give anecdotal accounts of how people began homeschooling and how they selected materials. They even include some war stories of what not to do. Books such as this one give an overview of educational and psychological research as it relates to homeschooling. This enables one to know what *should* work. The basic questions that should be answered before homeschooling are:

- Do we want a traditional or nontraditional curriculum?
- Who will be the primary teacher, and how do that person's personality characteristics mesh with the student's/students'?
- Do we want to teach for mastery, quantity of material, or somewhere between?
- What format will we use in our teaching (remember, it doesn't have to be the same for all subjects nor for the entire school year)?
- What are our beliefs about testing/evaluation?

- What types of rules will we have and how will they be enforced?
- What would be most motivating to our child/children?
- How will we set up the physical environment for homeschooling?
- Will we follow a strict schedule or be more relaxed in meeting the time requirements for homeschooling?

It is sometimes comforting to remember that throughout the ages children have been taught quite well at home. Only in the last century, and particularly in western civilizations, has there been such a universal use of mass schooling. It is my philosophy that there is no one who is as concerned about a child and that child's learning as his or her own parents. Who better to teach them? An appendix is included at the end of this book that contains material about curriculum publishers and helpful organizations.

APPENDIX:
ADDITIONAL RESOURCES
BY CHAPTER

CHAPTER 1: INFORMATION PROCESSING RESOURCES

www.exploratorium.org/memory/dont_forget/index.html (Memory Games)
www.mindtools.com/pages/main/newMN_TIM.htm (Memory Improvement Tools)

CHAPTER 2: ONLINE IQ TESTING

www.emode.com/tests/uiq (Emode.com)
www.intelligencetest.com (IQ Test Labs)
www.queendom.com/tests/iq/index.html (Queendom)

CHAPTER 3: ONLINE PERSONALITY TESTING

cac.psu.edu/~j5j/test/ipipneo1.htm (IPIP-NEO—International Personality Item Pool Representation of the NEO PI-R) The IPIP-NEO is a particularly good test that is free and available online as of this writing. It is geared toward adults, but it could also be used with high school students. It is a rather long test, so adequate time should be set aside, perhaps an hour or more.

CHAPTER 4: CURRICULUM SOURCES

www.aop.com (Alpha Omega Publications) "Switched-On Schoolhouse" is a computerized curriculum published by Alpha Omega Publishers. They also have paper curricula.

www.christianbook.com (Christian Book Distributors, or CBD) Although this is advertised as a Christian book site, they have a good cross section of just about everything a homeschooler might need.

www.bjup.com (Bob Jones University Press) This is a very academic, Christian-based curriculum. They have curriculum on satellite, video, books, and complete high school programs with diplomas; one can just pick and choose texts.

www.abeka.com (A Beka Books) All of A Beka's curriculum materials are infused with a Christian worldview. They were one of the first publishers to provide homeschooling materials. Some of the materials seem very simplistic, though some are quite good. Some of the teachers manuals are not very helpful.

www.thebackpack.com (The Backpack) This site advertises new and used homeschooling materials; some are used, some are not.

www.elijahco.com (Elijah Company) This company provides all types of homeschooling resources.

www.homeschoolfcgs.com (Farm Country General Store) This company provides all types of homeschooling resources.

www.greenleafpress.com/gleaf.htm (Greenleaf Press) Greenleaf sells literature-based curriculum materials.

www.sycamoretree.com (The Sycamore Tree Center for Home Education) This site provides homeschooling materials for purchase as well as online courses for homeschoolers.

CHAPTER 5

www.atozteacherstuff.com/tips/Motivating_Students (A to Z Teacher Stuff— Tips: Motivating Students) These are motivational techniques employed by classroom teachers. Many will transfer to the homeschooling environment.

CHAPTER 6

www.omnipotentchild.com (*The Omnipotent Child* by Thomas Millar) This book is perhaps the best childrearing and discipline book I've read. I use it in a senior-level university course titled "Managing Child Behavior."

www.nwrel.org/scpd/sirs/5/cu9.html ("Schoolwide and Classroom Discipline" by Kathleen Cotton) This is an excellent summary of classroom discipline research. Many ideas are given that transfer well to homeschooling situations. Ineffective practices are also discussed.

REFERENCES

Alpha Omega Publications. 2003. Switched-On Schoolhouse. Retrieved from www.aop.com.

Atkinson, J. W., and Feather, N. T., eds. 1966. *A theory of achievement motivation.* New York: Wiley.

Atkinson, R. C., and Shiffrin, R. M. 1968. Human memory: A proposed system and its control processes. Vol. 2 of *The psychology of learning and motivation: Advances in research and theory*, edited by K. W. Spence and J. T. Spence. San Diego, CA: Academic Press.

Ausubel, D., Novak, J., and Hanesian, H. (1978). *Educational psychology: A cognitive view.* New York: Holt, Rinehart, and Winston.

Bowman, J. S. 1979. The lecture-discussion format revisited. *Improving College and University Teaching* 27:25–27.

Cattell, R. B. 1963. Theory of fluid and crystallized intelligence: A critical experiment. *Journal of Educational Psychology* 54:1–22.

Childs, G. 1995. *Understand your temperament! A guide to the four temperaments: Choleric, sanguine, phlegmatic, melancholic.* Vancouver, BC: Sophia Books.

Core Knowledge Foundation. 2003. *Core Knowledge Sequence, K–8.* Retrieved from www.coreknowledge.org/CKproto2/bkstr/seqnc.htm.

Craik, F. I. M., and Lockhart, R. S. 1972. Levels of processing: A framework for memory research. *Journal of Verbal Learning and Verbal Behavior* 11:671–84.

Festinger, L. (1957). *A theory of cognitive dissonance*. Stanford, CA: Stanford University Press.

Gardner, H. 1993a. *Multiple intelligences: The theory in practice*. New York: Basic Books.

Gardner, H. 1993b. *Creating minds*. New York: Basic Books.

Guilford, J. P. 1967. *The nature of human intelligence*. New York: McGraw-Hill.

Horn, J. L. 1994. Theory of fluid and crystallized intelligence. In *Encyclopedia of intelligence*, edited by R. J. Sternberg. New York: Macmillan.

Horn, J. L., and Cattell, R. B. 1967. Refinement and test of the theory of fluid and crystallized ability intelligences. *Journal of Educational Psychology* 57:253–70.

Kounin, J. S. 1970. *Discipline and group management in classrooms*. New York: Holt, Rinehart and Winston.

LaHaye, T. 1984. *Why you act the way you do*. Wheaton, IL: Living Books.

Maslow, A. 1971. *The farther reaches of human nature*. New York: Viking.

McClelland, D.C. (1961). *The achieving society*. Princeton, N.J.: Van Nostrand.

Meeker, M. N. 1969. *The structure of intellect*. Columbus, OH: Merrill.

Murray, H. (1938, 1943). *Explorations in personality*. New York: Oxford University Press.

Piaget, J., and Inhelder, B. 1969. *The psychology of the child*. New York: Basic Books.

Saxon, J. 2001. *Advanced mathematics: An incremental development*. 2d ed. Norman, OK: Saxon Publishers, Inc.

Saxon, J., and Wang, F. 2002. *Calculus*. 2d ed. Norman, OK: Saxon Publishers, Inc.

Schonwetter, D. J. 1993. Attributes of effective lecturing in the college classroom. *Canadian Journal of Higher Education* 23:1–18.

Skinner, B. F. 1953. *Science and human behavior.* New York: Macmillan.

Spearman, C. 1904. General intelligence, objectively determined and measured. *American Journal of Psychology* 15:201–93.

Sternberg, R. J. 1990. *Metaphors of mind: Conceptions of the nature of intelligence*. New York: Cambridge University Press.

Sternberg, R. 1988. *The triarchic mind: A new theory of intelligence*. New York: Viking Press.

Thomas, A., and Chess, S. 1977. *Temperament and development*. New York: Brunner/Mazel.

Vygotsky, L. S. 1987. *The collected works of L. S. Vygotsky*, edited by R. W. Rieber and A. S. Carlton, vol. 3. New York: Plenum Press.

INDEX

ABOUT THE AUTHOR

Andrea D. Clements earned her Ph.D. in educational psychology from the University of Alabama in 1991. She has four children, whom she has homeschooled since 1998. The oldest has just begun college and the youngest is two years old. The others are five and fourteen. Her husband, Dale, who has been a private school teacher and administrator, is the primary homeschooling parent.

Dr. Clements teaches courses in educational psychology, developmental psychology, research methodology, and management of child behavior. Her research is in the area of exploring the physiological origins of children's behavior. She is currently investigating the relationship between childhood temperament and stress hormone levels.